# DATA STRUCTURES
# AND
# ALGORITHMS
# IN PYTHON

## Effective Coding and Smart Problem-Solving

MAXWELL RIVERS

# CONTENTS

# INTRODUCTION

## Why Learn Data Structures and Algorithms?

Imagine you're a chef in a busy kitchen. To create delicious dishes efficiently, you need the right tools – sharp knives, pots, pans, and a well-organized workspace. Similarly, in the world of programming, data structures and algorithms are your tools for creating efficient and powerful software.

## Efficiency Matters

Let's say you're building an app to find the shortest route between two locations. Without the right algorithms, your app might take forever to calculate routes, especially if you're dealing with a complex city map. But with the right algorithms, your app can quickly provide accurate directions, even for large and intricate maps.

Efficient algorithms are like well-optimized recipes. Just as a chef can cook more dishes in less time with the right techniques, a programmer can process and analyze data more quickly with the right algorithms. Learning these techniques can help you create software that's faster, uses less memory, and can handle larger amounts of data.

## Problem Solving and Creativity

Think of data structures and algorithms as the tools that help you solve puzzles and build intricate structures. When you encounter a problem, like sorting a list of names or finding the highest score in a game, algorithms provide step-by-step instructions for solving it. Data structures, on the other hand, help you organize and store data efficiently so that your algorithms can work their magic.

As you learn more about these concepts, you'll develop problem-solving skills that are applicable not only to programming but also to real-life challenges. Just like a puzzle enthusiast who becomes better at solving different kinds of puzzles, you'll become a more creative problem solver.

## Career Opportunities

The knowledge of data structures and algorithms is highly valued in the tech industry. Whether you're interested in software development, data science, artificial intelligence, or any other field involving programming, these concepts will be crucial to your success. Many tech companies use coding interviews to assess candidates' understanding of data structures and algorithms, so mastering these topics can give you a competitive edge in the job market.

Learning data structures and algorithms is like gaining a

superpower for programming. You'll be able to create software that's faster, smarter, and more efficient. Plus, you'll develop problem-solving skills that can benefit you in many aspects of life.

## Python's Role in Data Structures and Algorithms

Imagine you're embarking on a coding adventure, and Python is your trusty map and compass. Python is a programming language known for its simplicity and readability, making it an excellent companion as we navigate the world of data structures and algorithms.

Learning data structures and algorithms can seem daunting, but Python's straightforward syntax makes the journey much smoother. It's like having a language that speaks your thoughts – you can focus on understanding the concepts instead of deciphering complex code.

Python's elegant and natural style helps you express your ideas in fewer lines of code, saving you time and effort. Whether you're a coding newbie or an experienced developer, Python's simplicity accelerates your learning and problem-solving process.

Python comes with a treasure trove of built-in tools that align perfectly with our quest for mastering data structures and algorithms. These tools, known as data structures, include lists, tuples, dictionaries, and sets. Think of them as magical containers that hold your data in different ways, making it easier to manipulate and organize.

Let's not forget Python's array of functions and libraries that can handle common operations like sorting, searching, and manipulating strings. These functions are like shortcuts that save you from reinventing the wheel – instead, you can focus on understanding how these operations work under the hood.

Python's interactive nature lets you experiment and explore concepts in real time. You can write a few lines of code, run them, and immediately see the results. This hands-on approach accelerates your understanding of how data structures and algorithms function.

Additionally, Python has a vast and welcoming community. Countless online resources, tutorials, and forums are available to assist you when you stumble upon challenges. The supportive Python community ensures you're never alone on this exciting journey.

## Setting Up Your Development Environment

Let's set up our environment so that you're well-equipped for the exciting journey into data structures and algorithms.

### Choosing a Code Editor

A code editor is your virtual workspace where you'll write and edit your code. There are many code editors to choose from, both simple ones like Notepad and more advanced ones like Visual Studio Code. Visual Studio Code (VS Code) is popular among programmers for its user-friendly interface, extensions, and features tailored for various programming languages, including Python.

1. **Install Visual Studio Code:**
   - Go to the Visual Studio Code website.
   - Download the version that matches your operating system (Windows, macOS, or Linux).
   - Run the installer and follow the prompts.

## Installing Python

Python is the language we'll be using to explore data structures and algorithms. Before you can start coding in Python, you need to install it on your computer.

1. **Download Python:**
   - Visit the Python official website.
   - Click on the "Downloads" tab.
   - Choose the latest version for your operating system (Windows, macOS, or Linux).

2. **Run the Installer:**
   - Double-click the downloaded installer.
   - Check the box that says "Add Python x.x to PATH" (x.x represents the version number).
   - Click "Install Now."

## Creating Your First Python Program

Now that you have your development environment set up, let's write a simple Python program to make sure everything is working as expected.

1. **Open Visual Studio Code:**
   - Launch VS Code from your applications or start menu.

2. **Create a New Python File:**

   - Click "File" > "New File" to open a new blank file.

3. **Write Your Program:**

   - Type the following code into the file:

pythonCopy code

```
print("Hello, world!")
```

4. **Save the File:**

   - Click "File" > "Save As."

   - Choose a location on your computer and name the file with a **.py** extension (e.g., **hello.py**).

   - Click "Save."

5. **Run the Program:**

   - Open the integrated terminal in VS Code by clicking "View" > "Terminal."

   - Type **python hello.py** and press Enter.

Congratulations! You've just written and executed your first Python program. You're now ready to embark on your coding journey into the realm of data structures and algorithms.

# CHAPTER 1: PYTHON BASICS FOR DATA STRUCTURES AND ALGORITHMS

In this chapter, we'll lay the foundation by exploring the essential basics of Python programming. These are the building blocks that will help us understand and implement data structures and algorithms effectively.

**Variables and Data Types**

Imagine your computer's memory as a collection of labeled boxes where you can store different kinds of information. These labeled boxes are called variables. Variables can hold various types of data, such as numbers, text, and more.

For example, you can create a variable called name to store your name:

```
name = "Alice"
```

**Operators and Expressions**

Just like in math class, Python lets you use operators (+, -, *, /, etc.) to perform calculations. You can also combine values and variables to create expressions.

```
x = 5
y = 3
result = x + y * 2  # The result will be 11 (5 + 3 * 2)
```

### Control Structures: Conditional Statements and Loops

Conditional statements allow your program to make decisions. For instance, if you want to print a message only if a condition is met:

```
temperature = 25

if temperature > 20:
    print("It's a warm day!")
else:
    print("It's a bit chilly.")
```

Loops help you repeat actions. A common loop is the for loop:

```
for number in range(5):
    print(number)
```

### Functions and Scope

Functions are like reusable blocks of code. You can create functions to perform specific tasks and use them whenever needed.

```
def greet(name):
    print(f"Hello, {name}!")

greet("Bob")
```

Scope defines where a variable is accessible. Variables created inside a function have local scope and are only accessible within that function.

### Lists, Tuples, and Dictionaries

Lists are like containers that can hold multiple values. Tuples are similar to lists but are immutable, meaning their values can't be changed after creation. Dictionaries store key-value pairs.

```
fruits = ["apple", "banana", "cherry"]
coordinates = (10, 20)
person = {"name": "Alice", "age": 30}
```

## Variables and Data Types

Imagine your computer's memory as a big toolbox, and each box in the toolbox can hold something different – like numbers, words, or even pictures. Variables are like labels you put on these boxes so you can find them easily. In programming, variables help us store and manage different kinds of information.

### Naming Variables

When you create a variable, you give it a name that helps you remember what it holds. Just like naming your pet or your favorite toy! For example, if you want to remember your age, you can create a variable called **age**:

```
age = 25
```

### Data Types

Data types tell the computer what kind of information a variable holds. Here are some common data types:

1. **Numbers (Integers and Floats):**
   - Integers are whole numbers (e.g., 5, -10, 100).
   - Floats are numbers with decimal points (e.g., 3.14, -0.5).

```
age = 25 # This is an integer
temperature = 98.6 # This is a float
```

2. **Strings:**

   - Strings are sequences of characters, like words or sentences. They're enclosed in quotes.

```
name = "Alice"
message = "Hello, world!"
```

3. **Booleans:**

   - Booleans represent either **True** or **False**. They're often used for making decisions.

```
is_sunny = True
is_raining = False
```

## Changing and Reusing Variables

Just like you can put different things in a box, you can change the value stored in a variable whenever you want. For example:

```
name = "Alice"
name = "Bob" # Now the variable holds "Bob" instead of
"Alice"
```

## Type Conversion

Sometimes you might need to change a variable from one data type to another. For example, turning a number into a string:

```
number = 42
text_number = str(number) # Convert the number to a
string
```

## Operators and Expressions

Think of operators as magical symbols that let you perform different kinds of actions with your data. Just like + and - in math class, Python operators help you add, subtract, multiply, and do other cool things with numbers and other values.

### Arithmetic Operators

Arithmetic operators are like math helpers for your code. They let you do calculations with numbers:

- + Addition: Adds two numbers together.
- - Subtraction: Subtracts one number from another.
- * Multiplication: Multiplies two numbers.
- / Division: Divides one number by another.
- % Modulus: Gives the remainder after division.
- ** Exponentiation: Raises a number to a power.

```
x = 10
y = 3

sum_result = x + y # This will be 13
product_result = x * y # This will be 30
```

### Comparison Operators

Comparison operators help you compare values:

- == Equal to: Checks if two values are the same.
- != Not equal to: Checks if two values are different.
- < Less than: Checks if one value is smaller than another.
- > Greater than: Checks if one value is bigger than another.
- <= Less than or equal to: Checks if one value is smaller or equal.
- >= Greater than or equal to: Checks if one value is bigger or equal.

```
age = 25

is_adult = age >= 18 # This will be True, because 25 is
greater than 18
```

## Logical Operators

Logical operators help you combine different conditions:

- **and** Logical AND: Returns **True** if both conditions are **True**.
- **or** Logical OR: Returns **True** if at least one condition is **True**.
- **not** Logical NOT: Flips the value of a condition.

```
is_sunny = True
is_warm = True

is_nice_day = is_sunny and is_warm # This will be True,
because both conditions are True
```

### Expressions

An expression is like a small recipe that combines values, variables, and operators to create a result. For example:

```
total_cost = 20 + 5 # This is an expression that adds 20 and
5
```

## Control Structures: Conditional Statements and Loops

Imagine you're writing instructions for a robot. You want the robot to make decisions based on certain conditions and repeat actions until a task is complete. In programming, control structures like conditional statements and loops help you give instructions to your computer in a similar way.

### Conditional Statements

Conditional statements are like road signs for your code. They help your program make decisions and take different actions based on conditions.

- **if** statement: Executes a block of code if a condition is **True**.
- **else** statement: Provides an alternative block of code to execute if the **if** condition is not met.
- **elif** statement: Stands for "else if." You can use multiple **elif** statements to handle different conditions.

```
temperature = 25
```

```
if temperature > 20:
    print("It's a warm day!")
elif temperature <= 20:
    print("It's a bit chilly.")
```

## Loops

Loops are like the repeat button for your code. They let you execute a block of code multiple times.

- **for** loop: Repeats a block of code a specific number of times or for each item in a sequence (like a list).
- **while** loop: Repeats a block of code as long as a condition is **True**.

```
for number in range(5):
    print(number)  # This will print numbers from 0 to 4

count = 0
while count < 5:
    print("Hello!")
    count += 1  # Increase count by 1 in each iteration
```

## Break and Continue Statements

Inside loops, you can use **break** to exit the loop prematurely and **continue** to skip the current iteration and move to the next one.

```
for number in range(10):
    if number == 5:
        break  # Exit the loop when number is 5
    print(number)  # This will print numbers from 0 to 4
```

```
for number in range(5):
    if number == 2:
        continue  # Skip printing 2 and continue with the next
    iteration
    print(number)  # This will print numbers 0, 1, 3, 4
```

Control structures are the tools that allow your code to make decisions and repeat actions. Conditional statements guide your program's flow based on conditions, while loops enable you to automate tasks by executing a block of code multiple times. With these control structures, you can write code that adapts to different situations and performs repetitive tasks efficiently. Whether it's making decisions or looping through data, control structures are essential tools for any programmer.

## Functions and Scope

Imagine you have a magic spell that can do a specific task whenever you say its name. In programming, functions are like those magic spells – they let you group a set of instructions together and use them whenever you need them. Functions help you avoid repeating the same code and make your programs more organized.

### Creating Functions

Creating a function involves giving it a name and telling it what to do. Here's the basic structure of a function:

```
def greet(name):
```

```
print(f"Hello, {name}!")
```

- **def** keyword: This is used to define a function.
- **greet**: The name of the function.
- **(name)**: This is where you can give the function some information to work with (called parameters).

**Calling Functions**

Calling a function means using it to perform its task. In our example, you call the **greet** function like this:

```
greet("Alice") # This will print "Hello, Alice!"
```

**Returning Values**

Functions can also give you back a result after performing their task. For example:

```
def add(x, y):
    return x + y

result = add(5, 3)  # The result will be 8
```

**Scope**

Scope is like a boundary that determines where a variable can be used. Variables created inside a function have local scope, meaning they can only be used within that function. Variables created outside functions have global scope and can be used anywhere in the code.

```
def print_name():
    name = "Alice"
    print(name)  # This works because name is defined inside
the function

print_name()
# print(name)  # This would result in an error because
name is not defined here
```

Functions make your code organized and help you avoid repeating the same code over and over. Scope ensures that variables are used in the right places and don't interfere with each other. With functions and the concept of scope, you'll be able to create efficient and modular programs that perform tasks smoothly and without repetition.

## Lists, Tuples, and Dictionaries

Imagine you have a toolbox with compartments for storing different items. In programming, lists, tuples, and dictionaries are like your digital toolboxes, helping you organize and manage various types of data efficiently.

### Lists

A list is like a collection of items in a single container. You can have a list of numbers, words, or even a mix of different things.

```
fruits = ["apple", "banana", "cherry"]
numbers = [1, 2, 3, 4, 5]
mixed_list = [10, "apple", True]
```

- Lists are ordered: The items have a specific order, and you can access them using their positions (indices).

- Lists are mutable: You can change, add, or remove items after creating the list.

**Tuples**

A tuple is similar to a list, but it's like a fixed container – once you create it, you can't change the items inside.

```
coordinates = (10, 20)
person = ("Alice", 30, "Engineer")
```

- Tuples are ordered: Like lists, items have a specific order and can be accessed using indices.

- Tuples are immutable: You can't change the items in a tuple after creating it.

**Dictionaries**

A dictionary is like a special book where each word (key) has a definition (value). In programming, dictionaries help you store and retrieve data using unique keys.

```
person = {
  "name": "Alice",
  "age": 25,
  "occupation": "Engineer"
}
```

- Dictionaries are unordered: Items are not stored in any specific order.

- Dictionaries are mutable: You can change the values associated with keys.

## Accessing Items

You can access items in lists, tuples, and dictionaries using their indices or keys.

```
fruits = ["apple", "banana", "cherry"]
print(fruits[0]) # This will print "apple"

coordinates = (10, 20)
print(coordinates[1]) # This will print 20

person = {"name": "Alice", "age": 25}
print(person["name"]) # This will print "Alice"
```

Lists, tuples, and dictionaries are essential data structures that help you organize and manage data effectively in your Python programs. Lists allow you to group items in an ordered and mutable way, tuples provide a fixed and ordered collection, and dictionaries enable you to store data with meaningful keys for easy retrieval. By understanding and utilizing these data structures, you can handle a wide variety of data and create more powerful and organized programs.

# CHAPTER 2: UNDERSTANDING COMPLEXITY ANALYSIS

Welcome to the world of efficiency! In this chapter, we'll explore the concept of complexity analysis, which helps us understand how our algorithms perform as our input data grows larger. We'll delve into Big O notation, a powerful tool for comparing and analyzing the efficiency of different algorithms.

## The Importance of Efficiency

Imagine you're a busy chef in a restaurant kitchen. Your goal is to prepare delicious meals for all the hungry customers waiting. But there's a catch – you need to do it quickly, ensuring that everyone gets their food on time and nobody has to wait too long.

Similar to the kitchen scenario, efficiency plays a crucial role in the world of programming. An efficient program is like a skilled chef who can whip up dishes rapidly without sacrificing quality. Let's explore why efficiency matters and how it impacts the performance of your software.

## Speed Matters

In the digital age, speed is of the essence. Users expect software applications to respond swiftly, whether they're browsing the web, using a mobile app, or interacting with a desktop program. Efficient algorithms and well-optimized code contribute to faster execution times, leading to a smoother user experience.

Consider a web search engine. When you type a query and hit "Search," the engine needs to sift through vast amounts of data to provide you with relevant results. An efficient search algorithm ensures that you receive those results quickly, even when the search involves trillions of web pages.

## Resource Utilization

Efficient programs are also resource-friendly. They use system resources, such as memory and processing power, in a balanced and economical manner. Inefficient programs can hog resources, causing slowdowns or crashes, which frustrate users and negatively impact their experience.

Think of a smartphone app that drains your battery rapidly due to poor coding practices. Users might avoid using such an app altogether, affecting its popularity and reputation.

## Scalability and Growth

Efficiency becomes even more critical as your software grows. If your program is inefficient, it might struggle to handle larger datasets or more complex tasks. Efficient algorithms and code allow your software to scale gracefully, accommodating increasing demands without sacrificing performance.

Consider a social media platform. As the user base grows, an efficient platform can handle millions of users interacting simultaneously without becoming sluggish.

### Algorithmic Complexity

Behind efficient programs lie efficient algorithms. An algorithm's complexity determines how it performs as the input data increases. An algorithm with low complexity ensures that even as your data grows, the program remains responsive.

For example, in a video streaming app, an algorithm that quickly retrieves the next video to play based on user preferences ensures that viewers enjoy a seamless watching experience.

Efficiency isn't just a technical concept; it directly impacts user satisfaction, resource utilization, and the growth potential of your software. Efficient programs provide a snappy and responsive experience, optimize resource usage, and pave the way for scalability. By prioritizing efficiency in your coding practices and algorithm design, you're not just writing code – you're crafting high-performing solutions that enhance the user experience and drive the success of your projects.

## Big O Notation: A Primer

In the world of programming, efficiency is paramount. Imagine you're a conductor leading an orchestra, and you want every instrument to play harmoniously. Big O notation is like your sheet music – it helps you orchestrate your algorithms to perform optimally, no matter how complex the performance.

## Defining Big O Notation

Big O notation is a mathematical way to describe the performance of an algorithm. It tells you how the time or space requirements of an algorithm grow as the input size increases. In simpler terms, it helps you understand how efficient an algorithm is and how it handles larger amounts of data.

## Simplifying Complexities

Think of Big O notation as a shortcut to understanding an algorithm's efficiency. It abstracts away unnecessary details and focuses on the most significant factors that affect performance. This abstraction allows you to compare different algorithms quickly and make informed decisions about which one to use for a given task.

## Categories of Complexity

Big O notation categorizes algorithms based on their growth rates relative to the input size. Here are some common categories:

- **O(1)**: Constant Time Complexity. The time taken remains constant, regardless of the input size. Think of it as a single step.
- **O(log n)**: Logarithmic Time Complexity. The time taken increases slowly as the input size grows. Common in efficient search algorithms like binary search.
- **O(n)**: Linear Time Complexity. The time taken grows linearly with the input size. As the input doubles, the time

taken also doubles.

- **O(n log n)**: Linearithmic Time Complexity. Common in efficient sorting algorithms like merge sort and quick sort.
- **O(n^2)**: Quadratic Time Complexity. The time taken grows quadratically with the input size. As the input doubles, the time taken increases fourfold.
- **O(2^n)**: Exponential Time Complexity. Often seen in brute-force algorithms. Becomes inefficient rapidly as the input size increases.
- **O(n!)**: Factorial Time Complexity. Extremely inefficient for larger inputs. Often seen in algorithms that involve generating permutations.

## Why Big O Matters

Understanding Big O notation empowers you to choose the right algorithm for the job. Efficient algorithms ensure that your programs run smoothly, even with large datasets. It's like choosing the right tool for a task – a wrench for a bolt, a hammer for a nail. By selecting the appropriate algorithm based on Big O analysis, you're setting the stage for high-performance software.

Big O notation is your guide to algorithmic efficiency. It abstracts complex details and provides a clear picture of how an algorithm performs as the input size increases. This understanding allows you to make informed decisions, optimize your code, and create efficient solutions that tackle even the most complex computational challenges.

## Common Time Complexities

As you navigate various algorithms and their performances, knowing common time complexities helps you make informed decisions about which approach to take.

### O(1): Constant Time Complexity

Constant time complexity is like a magician's trick – it's lightning-fast, no matter the size of the input. Algorithms with O(1) complexity execute in the same amount of time regardless of how big the data is.

For example, accessing an element in an array by its index is O(1). It doesn't matter if the array has 10 or 10,000 elements; the time taken remains constant.

### O(log n): Logarithmic Time Complexity

Logarithmic time complexity is like narrowing down options in a game of "20 Questions." As the input size increases, the time taken to process it grows, but not dramatically. Algorithms with O(log n) complexity tend to divide the problem space in half with each step.

A classic example is binary search. When you're searching for a word in a dictionary, you keep dividing the word list in half until you find the right word. The larger the dictionary, the more efficient this approach becomes compared to linear search.

### O(n): Linear Time Complexity

Linear time complexity is like checking each item in a shopping list one by one. The time taken increases linearly as the input size grows. Algorithms with O(n) complexity scan through each element once.

For instance, finding the maximum value in an unsorted list requires inspecting every item. As the list gets longer, the time taken increases proportionally.

### O(n log n): Linearithmic Time Complexity

Linearithmic time complexity is like sorting playing cards using divide and conquer. Algorithms with O(n log n) complexity often involve breaking the data into smaller parts and then combining them.

Popular sorting algorithms like merge sort and quick sort fall into this category. These algorithms efficiently sort large amounts of data compared to quadratic time complexity algorithms like bubble sort.

### O(n^2): Quadratic Time Complexity

Quadratic time complexity is like cleaning every tile in a grid by visiting it row by row. The time taken increases quadratically as the input size grows. Algorithms with O(n^2) complexity often involve nested loops.

A simple example is the bubble sort algorithm, which repeatedly compares and swaps adjacent elements until the entire list is sorted. As the list grows, the number of comparisons and swaps increases dramatically.

Understanding common time complexities helps you gauge how algorithms perform as input sizes increase. This knowledge empowers you to choose the most suitable algorithm for your specific task, ensuring efficient execution and optimal resource usage. Just as a map guides a traveler, a grasp of time complexities guides you toward creating effective and responsive software solutions.

## Space Complexity Analysis

Imagine you're packing for a trip, and you need to fit everything you need into a single suitcase. In the world of programming, space complexity is like managing your suitcase space – it's about how much memory an algorithm uses to solve a problem. Efficient space usage is essential for creating programs that run smoothly and avoid wasting precious resources.

### What Is Space Complexity?

Space complexity is a measure of how much memory an algorithm requires as a function of the input size. Just as time complexity focuses on how long an algorithm takes to run, space complexity focuses on how much memory it consumes.

### Optimizing Memory Usage

Efficient space usage is crucial because memory is a finite resource. Inefficient programs that use excessive memory can slow down your system, lead to crashes, or affect the performance of other applications.

Consider a mobile app that stores user data. If the app consumes too much memory, it might lead to poor performance and battery drain, driving users away.

### Understanding Space Complexity Notation

Space complexity is typically denoted using Big O notation, just like time complexity. However, instead of analyzing the time it takes for an algorithm to run, you're analyzing the memory it uses.

For example, an algorithm with O(1) space complexity means that its memory usage remains constant regardless of the input size. An algorithm with O(n) space complexity means that its memory usage grows linearly with the input size.

### Trade-offs Between Time and Space Complexity

Efficiency is a balance between time and space. Some algorithms might be more memory-efficient but take longer to run, while others might be faster but consume more memory.

For instance, a trade-off often arises between using more memory to store precomputed values and achieving faster execution time. You might choose the approach that best aligns with your program's requirements and resource availability.

### Managing Memory Effectively

To optimize space usage, consider the following strategies:

1. **Avoid Unnecessary Data**: Store only the data you need. Don't waste memory on unnecessary variables or duplicate information.

2. **Use In-place Algorithms**: In-place algorithms modify the input data directly instead of creating additional data structures, saving memory.

3. **Recycle Memory**: Reuse memory space whenever possible. Avoid creating new memory blocks for every

operation.

4. **Use Data Structures Wisely**: Choose the right data structures for your task. Sometimes, using a more efficient data structure can reduce memory usage.

Space complexity analysis is like decluttering your programming suitcase. By understanding how much memory your algorithm uses, you can create more efficient programs that run smoothly and make the most of your available resources. Just as packing smartly leads to a hassle-free trip, optimizing memory usage leads to streamlined and resource-efficient software solutions.

# CHAPTER 3: ARRAYS AND STRINGS

Welcome to the heart of data manipulation! In this chapter, we'll dive deep into arrays and strings – fundamental data structures that allow you to store and manipulate collections of values. These building blocks form the foundation for solving a wide range of problems, from simple to complex.

## Introduction to Arrays

Imagine you're organizing a collection of books in a library. To make finding a specific book easier, you assign each book a unique number and place them on shelves in a specific order. In programming, arrays play a similar role – they help you manage collections of items in a structured and efficient way.

### What are Arrays?

An array is a data structure that allows you to store multiple values of the same data type in a single variable. Each value in an array is called an element, and each element is accessed using an index. Think of an array as a sequence of numbered storage compartments, each holding a specific value.

## Creating Arrays

To create an array in most programming languages, you use square brackets [] and separate the elements with commas:

```
numbers = [1, 2, 3, 4, 5]
names = ["Alice", "Bob", "Charlie"]
```

In this example, **numbers** is an array containing integers, and **names** is an array containing strings.

## Accessing Array Elements

Array elements are accessed using their indices, which start from 0. For example, to access the first element of the **numbers** array, you use **numbers[0]**. To access the second element, you use **numbers[1]**, and so on.

```
print(numbers[0]) # This will print 1
print(names[1]) # This will print "Bob"
```

## Array Size

The size of an array is the number of elements it contains. In some programming languages, arrays have a fixed size once they're created, while in others, you can dynamically change their size.

## Common Array Operations

Arrays support various operations, including:

- Adding Elements: You can add elements to an array using methods like **append()** or **insert()**.

- Updating Elements: Modify the value of an element by assigning a new value to it.

- Removing Elements: Delete elements using methods like **remove()** or **pop()**.

**Advantages of Arrays**

Arrays offer several benefits:

- **Efficient Access**: Array elements can be accessed directly using indices, making retrieval efficient.

- **Data Organization**: Arrays help organize related data in a structured manner.

- **Iterating**: You can easily loop through array elements to perform operations on each of them.

- **Memory Efficiency**: Arrays allow efficient memory allocation for storing large amounts of data.

Arrays are a foundational concept in programming, enabling you to manage collections of data efficiently. With arrays, you can organize related information, access elements quickly, and perform various operations on data. As you venture further into programming, understanding arrays will prove essential in solving diverse challenges and building robust applications.

## Basic Array Operations

Arrays are like Swiss Army knives in the programmer's toolkit

– they offer a wide range of capabilities for managing and manipulating collections of data.

## Adding Elements

Adding elements to an array is essential for building and expanding your data collection.

- **Appending**: You can add elements to the end of an array using the **append()** method:

```
numbers = [1, 2, 3]
numbers.append(4) # Adds 4 to the end of the array
```

- **Inserting**: To add an element at a specific position, use the **insert()** method:

```
names = ["Alice", "Bob", "Charlie"]
names.insert(1, "David") # Adds "David" at index 1, shifting
other elements
```

## Updating Elements

Updating elements allows you to modify the values in your array.

```
numbers = [1, 2, 3, 4, 5]
numbers[2] = 10 # Updates the third element to 10
```

## Removing Elements

Removing elements helps you keep your array clean and organized.

- **Using pop()**: The **pop()** method removes an element at a specific index and returns its value:

```
names = ["Alice", "Bob", "Charlie"]
removed_name = names.pop(1) # Removes "Bob" and
returns it
```

- **Using remove()**: The **remove()** method removes the first occurrence of a specified value:

```
fruits = ["apple", "banana", "cherry"]
fruits.remove("banana") # Removes the "banana" element
```

## Array Length

You can find the length (number of elements) of an array using the **len()** function:

```
numbers = [1, 2, 3, 4, 5]
length = len(numbers) # This will be 5
```

## Iterating Through Arrays

Looping through arrays allows you to perform actions on each element.

```
fruits = ["apple", "banana", "cherry"]
for fruit in fruits:
        print(fruit) # Prints each fruit in the array
```

## Finding Elements

You can check if a value exists in an array using the **in** keyword:

```
numbers = [1, 2, 3, 4, 5]
if 3 in numbers:
        print("3 is in the array")
```

Basic array operations empower you to build, modify, and manage collections of data efficiently. Whether you're adding, updating, or removing elements, these operations help you maintain order and structure in your programs. By understanding and utilizing these fundamental array techniques, you'll be well-equipped to tackle a wide range of programming challenges with confidence.

## Multidimensional Arrays

Imagine a chessboard – an 8x8 grid of squares. Each square can hold a piece like a pawn, a knight, or a king. In programming, multidimensional arrays allow you to create similar structures where data is organized in multiple dimensions. These arrays enable you to represent complex data relationships efficiently.

**What are Multidimensional Arrays?**

A multidimensional array is an array of arrays, where each element can also be an array. This arrangement creates a grid-like structure with rows and columns. In essence, it's an array of arrays, enabling you to store and manipulate data in two or more dimensions.

## Creating Multidimensional Arrays

In Python, you can create a two-dimensional array using nested lists:

```python
matrix = [
        [1, 2, 3],
        [4, 5, 6],
        [7, 8, 9]
]
```

In this example, **matrix** is a 3x3 two-dimensional array.

## Accessing Elements

Accessing elements in a multidimensional array requires specifying both the row and column indices:

```python
value = matrix[1][2] # This will retrieve the value 6
```

## Working with Multidimensional Arrays

Multidimensional arrays are versatile and suitable for various applications:

- **Matrix Operations**: Matrices can be used for mathematical operations, such as matrix multiplication and transformation.
- **Image Processing**: Images can be represented as multidimensional arrays of pixel values.
- **Board Games**: Multidimensional arrays can model game boards for chess, tic-tac-toe, and more.
- **Tabular Data**: Multidimensional arrays can be used to

represent spreadsheet-like data.

## Iterating Through Multidimensional Arrays

Nested loops are often used to iterate through multidimensional arrays:

```
matrix = [
        [1, 2, 3],
        [4, 5, 6],
        [7, 8, 9]
]

for row in matrix:
        for element in row:
                print(element)
```

## Three-Dimensional Arrays

While two-dimensional arrays represent a grid, three-dimensional arrays add another layer of complexity, allowing you to organize data in three dimensions. Think of a three-dimensional array as a stack of matrices.

Multidimensional arrays provide a powerful way to organize and manipulate data that has more than one dimension. Whether you're dealing with grids, images, or complex data structures, understanding and utilizing multidimensional arrays enables you to model and process information efficiently. These arrays form a bridge to understanding and solving problems involving intricate data relationships in various fields of programming and beyond.

## Strings and Manipulation

Strings are like the storytellers of the programming world – they convey messages, information, and text-based data. But strings are more than just words; they're versatile data types that can be manipulated and transformed in various ways to suit your needs.

### What are Strings?

A string is a sequence of characters. Characters can be letters, numbers, symbols, or spaces. In programming, strings are used to represent text-based data.

### Creating Strings

You can create strings by enclosing text in single (' ') or double (" ") quotes:

```
message = "Hello, world!"
name = 'Alice'
```

### String Concatenation

String concatenation involves combining two or more strings to form a longer string:

```
greeting = "Hello"
name = "Alice"
message = greeting + ", " + name # This will be "Hello, Alice"
```

### String Length

To find the length of a string (the number of characters), you can use the **len()** function:

```
text = "Python is fun!"
length = len(text) # This will be 14
```

## String Indexing and Slicing

You can access individual characters in a string using their indices:

```
text = "Python"
first_character = text[0] # This will be "P"
second_character = text[1] # This will be "y"
```

You can also slice strings to extract substrings:

```
text = "Python is great"
substring = text[0:6] # This will be "Python"
```

## String Methods

Strings come with a plethora of built-in methods for manipulation:

- **upper()**: Converts the string to uppercase.
- **lower()**: Converts the string to lowercase.
- **replace()**: Replaces occurrences of a substring with another substring.
- **strip()**: Removes leading and trailing whitespace.
- **split()**: Splits the string into a list of substrings based on a delimiter.

```
sentence = "Python is fun"
uppercase_sentence = sentence.upper() # "PYTHON IS
FUN"
replaced_sentence = sentence.replace("fun", "amazing") #
"Python is amazing"
```

### String Formatting

String formatting lets you create dynamic strings by inserting values into placeholders:

```
name = "Alice"
age = 30
message = f"Hello, my name is {name} and I am {age} years
old."
```

Strings are essential tools for representing and manipulating textual data. From concatenation and slicing to using various string methods, you can transform strings to suit your programming needs. Strings are not just lines of text; they're dynamic entities that allow you to create, edit, and convey information effectively. By mastering string manipulation, you unlock a world of possibilities for creating interactive and user-friendly applications.

## String Algorithms: Anagrams, Palindromes, and Patterns

Strings are more than just sequences of characters – they can hold secrets, patterns, and hidden messages.

### Anagrams: Rearranging Letters

Anagrams are words or phrases formed by rearranging the letters of another word or phrase. For example, "listen" and "silent" are anagrams. Anagram algorithms involve comparing the frequency of characters in two strings to determine if they can be rearranged into each other.

### Palindrome: Symmetrical Delight

A palindrome is a word, phrase, number, or other sequence of characters that reads the same forward and backward. Examples include "radar," "madam," and "level." Palindrome algorithms check if a given string remains the same when its characters are reversed.

### Pattern Matching: Finding Substrings

Pattern matching algorithms help find occurrences of a specified pattern (substring) within a larger string. This is a fundamental operation in text processing, data parsing, and search applications.

- **Brute Force**: The simplest approach is to iterate through the text and check if the pattern matches at each position. This is effective for small patterns but can be inefficient for larger texts.

- **KMP Algorithm**: The Knuth-Morris-Pratt algorithm uses a prefix function to optimize pattern matching by avoiding unnecessary comparisons.

- **Boyer-Moore Algorithm**: This algorithm skips characters based on the pattern and the text, leading to efficient pattern matching, especially for longer patterns.

## String Algorithms in Python

Here's a simple example of checking if a string is a palindrome in Python:

```python
def is_palindrome(s):
        s = s.lower().replace(" ", "") # Convert to lowercase
and remove spaces
        return s == s[::-1] # Compare with its reverse

word = "level"
if is_palindrome(word):
        print(f"{word} is a palindrome.")
else:
        print(f"{word} is not a palindrome.")
```

## Real-World Applications

- Anagrams and palindromes are often used in word games, cryptography, and linguistic analysis.
- Pattern matching algorithms power search engines, compilers, and data extraction tools.
- DNA sequence analysis involves identifying patterns and similarities in genetic data.

String algorithms go beyond characters; they reveal fascinating properties and patterns in text-based data. By understanding and implementing algorithms for anagrams, palindromes, and pattern matching, you gain insights into the structure and relationships within strings. These algorithms are not just for linguistics and puzzles – they're essential tools for solving real-world problems, from data analysis to coding interviews.

# CHAPTER 4: LINKED LISTS

Welcome to the world of dynamic data structures! In this chapter, we'll explore linked lists – a fundamental data structure that offers flexibility in storing and organizing data. Linked lists are like a chain of interconnected nodes, and they provide the basis for more complex data structures like stacks, queues, and more.

## Introduction to Linked Lists

Imagine a chain of interconnected beads, each holding a unique color. In programming, linked lists function similarly – they are dynamic data structures that consist of nodes, each holding an element and a reference to the next node in the sequence. Linked lists provide a flexible and efficient way to organize and manage data.

### What are Linked Lists?

A linked list is a collection of nodes, where each node contains two parts: data and a reference (or link) to the next node. The order of nodes in a linked list is determined by these references, creating a sequence.

**Advantages of Linked Lists**

Linked lists offer several advantages:

- **Dynamic Size**: Linked lists can grow or shrink dynamically as elements are added or removed.

- **Efficient Insertions and Deletions**: Inserting or deleting an element involves changing references, which is often faster than shifting elements in an array.

- **Memory Flexibility**: Nodes in a linked list can be scattered in memory, unlike arrays, which require contiguous memory allocation.

**Types of Linked Lists**

There are different types of linked lists, each with unique characteristics:

- **Singly Linked List**: Each node contains data and a reference to the next node.

- **Doubly Linked List**: Each node has references to both the next and previous nodes, allowing traversal in both directions.

- **Circular Linked List**: The last node points back to the first node, forming a closed loop.

**Creating Linked Lists**

Linked lists are typically implemented using classes. Each node is an instance of the node class, and the linked list class manages the nodes.

```
class Node:
    def __init__(self, data):
        self.data = data
        self.next = None

class LinkedList:
    def __init__(self):
        self.head = None
```

## Linked Lists vs. Arrays

Arrays are contiguous blocks of memory, while linked lists consist of scattered nodes. Linked lists are advantageous for insertions and deletions, while arrays offer faster access times for elements.

## Real-World Applications

- Linked lists are used in many programming languages' internal data structures for memory management.
- They're employed in various algorithms for their efficiency in certain operations.
- They're a crucial building block for more complex data structures like stacks, queues, and hash tables.

Linked lists are a powerful tool in the programmer's toolkit, offering a dynamic and efficient way to organize and manage data. By understanding their structure, types, and advantages, you'll be better equipped to utilize linked lists for various programming tasks. Whether you're managing data, optimizing algorithms, or building more advanced data structures, linked lists provide the foundation for flexible and effective solutions.

## Singly Linked Lists: Implementation and Operations

### Understanding Singly Linked Lists

A singly linked list is a linear data structure where each element (node) contains both data and a reference (link) to the next node in the sequence. The last node points to **None**, indicating the end of the list.

### Creating a Singly Linked List

To implement a singly linked list, you need a **Node** class to create nodes and a **LinkedList** class to manage the list.

```python
class Node:
    def __init__(self, data):
        self.data = data
        self.next = None

class LinkedList:
    def __init__(self):
        self.head = None
```

### Insertion Operations

Singly linked lists shine when it comes to insertion operations, as they can be performed efficiently:

- **Inserting at the Beginning**: This involves creating a new node, updating its **next** reference to the current head, and making the new node the new head.

- **Inserting at the End**: Traverse the list to find the last node, then update its **next** reference to the new node.
- **Inserting in the Middle**: Locate the node after which you want to insert, update the **next** reference of the new node, and adjust the references of surrounding nodes.

## Deletion Operations

Singly linked lists also offer efficient deletion operations:

- **Deleting the First Node**: Update the head to point to the second node, effectively skipping the first node.
- **Deleting the Last Node**: Traverse the list until the node before the last one, then update its **next** reference to **None**.
- **Deleting a Node in the Middle**: Locate the node before the one you want to delete, update its **next** reference to skip the node to be deleted.

## Traversal and Searching

To traverse a singly linked list, you can follow the **next** references starting from the head. Searching for a specific element involves traversing the list until the desired element is found or reaching the end.

## Advantages and Disadvantages

Advantages of singly linked lists include efficient insertion and deletion, dynamic size, and memory flexibility. However, they may not offer constant-time access to elements like arrays.

## Real-World Applications

- Singly linked lists are used in implementations of stacks, queues, and hash tables.

- They're used in memory management for garbage collection and dynamic memory allocation.
- Some programming languages use linked lists for their internal data structures.

Singly linked lists provide a dynamic and efficient way to organize and manipulate data. By understanding their structure and mastering insertion, deletion, traversal, and searching operations, you'll have a valuable tool at your disposal for various programming challenges. Whether you're building data structures, optimizing algorithms, or managing memory, singly linked lists offer the flexibility and efficiency needed to tackle a wide range of tasks.

## Doubly Linked Lists: Implementation and Advantages

### Understanding Doubly Linked Lists

A doubly linked list is a linear data structure in which each element (node) contains data and references to both the next and previous nodes. This bidirectional linking allows for efficient traversal in both directions.

### Creating a Doubly Linked List

To implement a doubly linked list, you need a **Node** class with references to the previous and next nodes, and a **DoublyLinkedList** class to manage the list.

```python
class Node:
    def __init__(self, data):
        self.data = data
        self.prev = None
        self.next = None

class DoublyLinkedList:
    def __init__(self):
        self.head = None
        self.tail = None
```

## Insertion and Deletion Operations

Doubly linked lists offer similar insertion and deletion operations to singly linked lists, but with the added advantage of bidirectional traversal:

- **Insertion**: Inserting at the beginning, end, or middle involves updating both the **next** and **prev** references of adjacent nodes.
- **Deletion**: Deletion operations require updating references of adjacent nodes to bypass the node being deleted.

## Advantages of Doubly Linked Lists

Doubly linked lists provide several advantages over singly linked lists:

- **Bidirectional Traversal**: Doubly linked lists allow traversal in both directions, which can be advantageous for certain operations.
- **Efficient Deletion**: Deleting a node in a doubly linked list can be more efficient than in a singly linked list since you have references to both the previous and next nodes.

- **Reverse Traversal**: Reverse traversal becomes straightforward due to the bidirectional links.

**Real-World Applications**

- Doubly linked lists are commonly used in applications requiring reverse traversal, such as text editors and browsers for managing history.

- They're useful in certain algorithms, like implementing LRU (Least Recently Used) caching policies.

- Some programming languages use doubly linked lists for their internal data structures.

Doubly linked lists enhance the capabilities of linked list data structures by allowing bidirectional traversal and efficient deletion operations. By understanding their implementation and advantages, you can leverage doubly linked lists to efficiently manage and manipulate data. Whether you're building data structures, optimizing algorithms, or implementing specific functionality like reverse traversal, doubly linked lists provide a versatile tool that opens up new possibilities for your programming endeavors.

## Circular Linked Lists: A Circular Approach to Data

Imagine a merry-go-round – a never-ending loop that keeps spinning. Circular linked lists are like that, creating a loop of interconnected nodes where the last node points back to the first.

### Understanding Circular Linked Lists

A circular linked list is a variation of linked lists where the last node points back to the first node, forming a closed loop. This loop-like structure can have applications in scenarios requiring continuous cycling through elements.

### Creating a Circular Linked List

To implement a circular linked list, you need a **Node** class similar to the one used for singly or doubly linked lists, but with an adjustment to the last node's reference.

pythonCopy code

class Node: def __init__(self, data): self.data = data self.next = None class CircularLinkedList: def __init__(self): self.head = None

### Insertion and Deletion Operations

Insertion and deletion operations in a circular linked list are similar to those in singly or doubly linked lists, with the additional consideration of the circular structure:

- **Insertion**: When inserting nodes, ensure that the new node's **next** reference points to the first node, thus closing the loop.

- **Deletion**: Deletion operations require updating references as usual, taking care not to break the circular structure.

### Advantages of Circular Linked Lists

Circular linked lists offer unique advantages:

- **Continuous Cycling**: Circular linked lists are useful when you need to cycle through elements indefinitely.

- **Efficient Operations**: Operations like insertion and deletion can be efficient in circular linked lists, similar to other linked list types.

- **Circular Queues**: Circular linked lists can be used to implement circular queues, which are commonly used in data buffering.

**Real-World Applications**

- Circular linked lists are used in applications like music playlists, where songs loop back to the beginning after the last song.
- They're also employed in scheduling algorithms, where processes repeat in a cyclical manner.
- Some memory management algorithms and operating systems use circular linked lists.

Circular linked lists provide a unique perspective on linked list data structures, offering a loop-like structure that can be useful for various applications. By understanding their implementation and advantages, you can leverage circular linked lists to create data structures that cycle through elements, emulate circular queues, and efficiently manage and manipulate data. Whether you're dealing with playlists, scheduling, or memory management, circular linked lists offer a powerful tool for creating dynamic and cyclical data structures.

## Practical Use Cases of Linked Lists

Linked lists, with their dynamic and efficient data storage and manipulation, find a wide array of practical applications in various domains.

## 1. Dynamic Memory Allocation

Linked lists are used in memory management systems to allocate and deallocate memory blocks dynamically. They help avoid memory fragmentation and allow for efficient allocation of memory of varying sizes.

## 2. Music and Video Playlists

Playlists in music and video streaming applications utilize linked lists to manage the sequence of songs or videos. Linked lists provide the flexibility to add, remove, and shuffle elements in the playlist with ease.

## 3. Undo and Redo Operations

In text editors, graphic design tools, and software applications, linked lists are employed to implement undo and redo functionality. Each change made to the data is recorded as a node in the linked list, allowing users to traverse back and forth through their actions.

## 4. Navigation Systems

GPS navigation systems utilize linked lists to represent road networks and routes. Nodes in the linked list correspond to intersections or waypoints, and the references between nodes determine the available paths and directions.

## 5. Task Scheduling

Operating systems use linked lists to manage various system processes and tasks. Ready queues, waiting queues, and process control blocks can be implemented using linked lists, allowing efficient scheduling and management of processes.

## 6. Hash Tables

Some implementations of hash tables use linked lists to handle collisions. If two elements hash to the same index, they're stored as nodes in the linked list associated with that index.

## 7. Symbol Tables in Compilers

In compiler design, symbol tables store information about variables, functions, and other program entities. Linked lists can be used to manage the entries in these symbol tables efficiently.

## 8. Browser History

Web browsers maintain a history of visited web pages. This history can be implemented as a linked list, where each page visit creates a new node that points to the previous and next pages visited.

## 9. Expression Evaluation

Linked lists can be used to convert infix expressions (e.g., "2 + 3 * 4") to postfix expressions (e.g., "2 3 4 * +"), which are easier to evaluate using a stack.

## 10. Memory Caching

In cache memory management, the least recently used (LRU) algorithm can be implemented using a linked list. Nodes represent cache items, and the order of nodes indicates their recent usage.

Linked lists are versatile data structures with practical applications across various domains. Their dynamic nature, efficient insertion and deletion, and ability to represent relationships between elements make them valuable tools for solving real-world problems. From memory management to playlists, from navigation systems to scheduling algorithms, linked lists continue to play a vital role in modern software development, offering flexibility and efficiency in managing and manipulating data.

# CHAPTER 5: STACKS AND QUEUES

Welcome to the world of linear data structures that add order and organization to your programming toolbox. In this chapter, we'll explore two essential data structures – stacks and queues – that enable you to manage data in a structured and efficient manner.

## Understanding Stacks and Queues

In the world of data structures, stacks and queues play a fundamental role in managing and organizing data in a structured manner. These linear data structures follow specific rules for adding and removing elements, and they find applications in a wide range of algorithms and real-world scenarios.

### Stacks: Last-In-First-Out (LIFO)

Imagine a stack of plates – the last plate you place is the first one you'll remove. This is the essence of a stack, following the Last-In-First-Out (LIFO) principle. In a stack, the most recently added element is the one that will be accessed and removed first.

**Stack Operations:**

1. **Push**: Adding an element to the top of the stack.

2. **Pop**: Removing and retrieving the top element from the stack.

3. **Peek**: Viewing the top element without removing it.

**Use Cases of Stacks:**

- **Function Call Tracking**: Stacks are used to keep track of function calls and return addresses in programming languages.

- **Expression Evaluation**: Stacks help evaluate arithmetic expressions by converting them to postfix notation.

- **Undo/Redo Functionality**: Stacks are employed to implement undo and redo operations in applications.

- **Backtracking Algorithms**: Stacks assist in backtracking algorithms like depth-first search.

**Queues: First-In-First-Out (FIFO)**

Imagine standing in line at a ticket counter – the person who arrives first gets served first. This is the basis of a queue, following the First-In-First-Out (FIFO) principle. In a queue, the element that has been in the queue the longest is the one that will be removed first.

**Queue Operations:**

1. **Enqueue**: Adding an element to the back of the queue.

2. **Dequeue**: Removing and retrieving the front element from the queue.

## Use Cases of Queues:

- **Task Scheduling**: Queues are essential for scheduling tasks and managing resources.

- **Breadth-First Search**: Queues are used in algorithms that explore a graph in breadth-first order.

- **Print Queue**: In printers, documents are processed in the order they're received.

- **Managing Resources**: Queues can control access to resources, ensuring fairness.

## Special Variants:

- **Circular Queue**: A queue that wraps around in a circular manner to efficiently utilize limited space.

- **Priority Queue**: A type of queue where elements have assigned priorities, and the highest-priority element is dequeued first.

## Real-World Analogy

Imagine a cafeteria line – people join at the end, get served from the front, and leave from there. This resembles the operation of a queue. For a stack, think of a stack of trays – you add trays from the top and remove them from there.

Stacks and queues are foundational concepts in computer science and programming. By understanding their principles, operations, and use cases, you'll be well-equipped to apply them in solving various problems and building more efficient and organized algorithms. These linear data structures provide valuable tools for managing data and controlling processes in diverse applications across the programming landscape.

## Implementing Stacks in Python

A stack is a fundamental data structure that follows the Last-In-First-Out (LIFO) principle. It's like a stack of plates – the last plate you place is the first one you'll remove.

### Using Lists as Stacks

Python's built-in list data structure can be easily used to implement a stack. The **append()** method adds elements to the end of the list, and the **pop()** method removes and returns the last element, effectively implementing a stack.

```
stack = []  # Initialize an empty list as a stack

# Push elements onto the stack
stack.append(10)
stack.append(20)
stack.append(30)

# Pop elements from the stack
top_element = stack.pop()  # This will be 30
```

### Using Collections.deque

The **collections** module in Python provides a double-ended queue (deque) that can be used to implement a stack. Deques are efficient for adding and removing elements from both ends.

```python
from collections import deque

stack = deque()  # Initialize an empty deque as a stack

# Push elements onto the stack
stack.append(10)
stack.append(20)
stack.append(30)

# Pop elements from the stack
top_element = stack.pop()  # This will be 30
```

## Implementing a Stack Class

You can also create a custom stack class using a linked list structure. Here's a basic example:

```python
class StackNode:
    def __init__(self, data):
        self.data = data
        self.next = None

class Stack:
    def __init__(self):
        self.top = None

    def push(self, data):
        new_node = StackNode(data)
        new_node.next = self.top
        self.top = new_node

    def pop(self):
        if self.top:
            popped_data = self.top.data
            self.top = self.top.next
```

```
        return popped_data
    else:
        return None
```

**Real-World Applications**

- Stacks are used for function call tracking in programming languages.
- They play a role in undo/redo functionality in applications.
- Expression evaluation and backtracking algorithms utilize stacks.

Implementing stacks in Python can be achieved using built-in lists, collections.deque, or by creating a custom stack class. Regardless of the approach, understanding how stacks work and their various applications is crucial for effective problem-solving and algorithm development. Stacks offer a structured and efficient way to manage data, making them an essential tool in the programmer's toolkit.

## Implementing Queues in Python

Queues are versatile data structures that follow the First-In-First-Out (FIFO) principle – the first element added is the first one to be removed. They resemble lines at a ticket counter, where the person who arrives first gets served first.

### Using Lists as Queues

While Python lists can be used to implement queues, they are not the most efficient option due to the overhead of shifting elements when using the **pop(0)** method. However, you can still simulate a queue with a list using **append()** to enqueue and **pop(0)** to dequeue.

```
queue = []  # Initialize an empty list as a queue

# Enqueue elements into the queue
queue.append(10)
queue.append(20)
queue.append(30)

# Dequeue elements from the queue
front_element = queue.pop(0)  # This will be 10
```

### Using collections.deque

Python's **collections** module provides a double-ended queue (deque) that is well-suited for implementing queues. Deques efficiently handle adding and removing elements from both ends.

```
from collections import deque

queue = deque()  # Initialize an empty deque as a queue

# Enqueue elements into the queue
queue.append(10)
queue.append(20)
queue.append(30)

# Dequeue elements from the queue
front_element = queue.popleft()  # This will be 10
```

### Implementing a Queue Class

You can create a custom queue class using a linked list structure. Here's a basic example:

```python
class QueueNode:
    def __init__(self, data):
        self.data = data
        self.next = None

class Queue:
    def __init__(self):
        self.front = None
        self.rear = None

    def enqueue(self, data):
        new_node = QueueNode(data)
        if not self.front:
            self.front = new_node
            self.rear = new_node
        else:
            self.rear.next = new_node
            self.rear = new_node

    def dequeue(self):
        if self.front:
            removed_data = self.front.data
            self.front = self.front.next
            if not self.front:
                self.rear = None
            return removed_data
        else:
            return None
```

## Real-World Applications

- Queues are used in task scheduling and managing

resources.

- They play a critical role in breadth-first search algorithms.
- Print queues in printers ensure documents are processed in order.

Implementing queues in Python can be achieved using built-in lists (with performance trade-offs) or using the more efficient **collections.deque**. You can also create a custom queue class using a linked list structure. Understanding how to implement and utilize queues is crucial for tasks that involve managing ordered data, scheduling, and algorithmic operations. Queues provide an organized and efficient way to process data in the order it arrives, making them invaluable tools in various programming scenarios.

## Applications of Stacks and Queues

Stacks and queues are versatile data structures that find applications in a wide range of domains and programming scenarios. They provide organized ways to manage data, control processes, and solve complex problems efficiently.

**Applications of Stacks:**

1. **Function Call Tracking**: Stacks are used to track function calls and manage the order in which they are executed. When a function is called, its information is pushed onto the stack, and when it returns, it's popped off the stack.

2. **Expression Evaluation**: Stacks play a vital role in evaluating arithmetic expressions. They are used to convert

infix expressions to postfix notation, making the evaluation process more efficient.

3. **Undo/Redo Functionality**: Stacks are employed in applications that require undo and redo functionality. Each action is pushed onto the stack, allowing users to reverse or redo their actions.

4. **Backtracking Algorithms**: Algorithms that involve backtracking, like depth-first search, use stacks to keep track of the paths or decisions made.

5. **Browser History**: Stacks are used to maintain the history of visited web pages. Each page visit is pushed onto the stack, allowing users to navigate backward through their browsing history.

6. **Memory Management**: Stacks are utilized in memory management for function call stacks and managing local variables.

7. **Expression Parsing**: Stacks are employed in parsing and evaluating expressions, such as parsing JSON or XML data.

**Applications of Queues:**

1. **Task Scheduling**: Queues are crucial in scheduling tasks and managing resources. They ensure tasks are executed in the order they were received.

2. **Breadth-First Search (BFS)**: Queues are used in BFS algorithms to explore a graph or tree level by level, making them useful for shortest path and graph traversal problems.

3. **Print Queue**: Printers use queues to manage print jobs in the order they are sent. The first print job received is the first to be printed.

4. **Buffer Management**: Queues are used to manage data in buffers, ensuring data is processed in the order it arrives.

5. **Call Center Systems**: Queues are employed to manage incoming customer requests, ensuring they are processed in the order they are received.

6. **Transaction Processing**: Queues are used in systems that process transactions, ensuring that transactions are executed in the order they are submitted.

7. **Synchronization and Parallelism**: Queues are used in concurrent programming to synchronize and coordinate tasks between different threads or processes.

Stacks and queues are foundational data structures that find applications in diverse fields such as programming, software development, algorithms, data processing, and system design. By understanding their characteristics and applications, you can effectively leverage these data structures to solve problems, optimize algorithms, and create efficient and organized solutions. From managing function calls to scheduling tasks, from evaluating expressions to processing data streams, stacks and queues are essential tools that play a significant role in the world of computer science and programming.

# CHAPTER 6: RECURSION AND BACKTRACKING

Welcome to the captivating world of recursion and backtracking – two powerful techniques that unlock elegant solutions to complex problems. In this chapter, we'll delve into the concepts of recursion and backtracking, exploring how they work, when to use them, and how they can help you tackle intricate challenges.

## Recursive Thinking and Problem Solving

Recursive thinking is a powerful mental approach that allows you to break down complex problems into simpler, more manageable components. Just as a puzzle can be solved by solving smaller pieces, recursive thinking enables you to tackle intricate challenges by solving smaller versions of the same problem.

### The Essence of Recursion

At its core, recursion involves solving a problem by reducing it to one or more smaller instances of the same problem. This reduction continues until the problem reaches a base case – the simplest form of the problem that can be solved directly. Recursive solutions often consist of two main components:

1.  **Base Case**: A condition that specifies when the problem is simple enough to be solved directly without further recursion.

2.  **Recursive Case**: A step that breaks down the problem into smaller instances, often by calling the same function with modified parameters.

**Recursive Thinking in Action: Fibonacci Sequence**

The Fibonacci sequence is a classic example of recursion. Each number in the sequence is the sum of the two preceding numbers: 0, 1, 1, 2, 3, 5, 8, ...

```python
def fibonacci(n):
    if n == 0:
        return 0
    elif n == 1:
        return 1
    else:
        return fibonacci(n - 1) + fibonacci(n - 2)
```

**Guidelines for Recursive Problem Solving**

1.  **Identify Base Cases**: Determine the simplest instances of the problem that can be solved directly. Base cases stop the recursion.

2.  **Define Recursive Cases**: Determine how to break down the problem into smaller instances. This often involves

calling the same function with modified parameters.

3. **Use Recursion**: Apply the recursive approach to solve the smaller instances, moving closer to the base case.

4. **Combine Solutions**: Combine the solutions of the smaller instances to solve the original problem.

## Benefits of Recursive Thinking

- **Elegance**: Recursive solutions can be more elegant and concise than iterative ones, capturing the essence of the problem.

- **Complexity Management**: Recursive thinking simplifies complex problems by reducing them to smaller, manageable parts.

- **Versatility**: Recursive techniques can be applied to a wide range of problems, from mathematical sequences to tree traversal.

## Challenges and Considerations

- **Time and Space Complexity**: Recursive solutions can sometimes result in higher time and space complexity compared to iterative solutions.

- **Stack Overflow**: Poorly designed recursive algorithms may lead to a stack overflow due to excessive function calls.

## Real-World Applications

- Tree and graph traversal algorithms often use recursion to explore nodes and edges.

- Divide and conquer algorithms like merge sort and

quicksort employ recursive thinking.

Recursive thinking is a powerful approach that transforms complex problems into solvable pieces. By identifying base cases, defining recursive cases, and applying the process iteratively, you can tackle intricate challenges more effectively. Recursive thinking provides a deeper understanding of problem structures, enabling you to craft elegant and efficient solutions. From mathematics to computer science, mastering recursive thinking is a valuable skill that empowers you to solve a wide variety of problems with clarity and creativity.

## Recursive vs. Iterative Approaches

In the realm of problem-solving and algorithm development, two primary strategies emerge: recursion and iteration. Both approaches aim to achieve the same goal – solving complex problems – but they do so in distinct ways.

**Recursive Approach:**

**Strengths:**

1. **Elegance**: Recursive solutions often mirror the problem's structure, resulting in elegant and concise code that captures the problem's essence.

2. **Divide and Conquer**: Recursive thinking breaks down complex problems into smaller, manageable pieces, enabling a divide-and-conquer strategy.

3. **Complex Structures**: Recursion is ideal for problems

involving complex structures like trees, graphs, and recursive data types.

**Weaknesses:**

1. **Stack Usage**: Recursion typically uses the call stack, which may lead to stack overflow errors if not managed properly.

2. **Performance Overhead**: Recursive function calls can introduce performance overhead due to the repeated function call overhead.

3. **Time and Space Complexity**: In some cases, recursive solutions might have higher time and space complexity compared to iterative counterparts.

**When to Use Recursion:**

- Problems that can be naturally divided into smaller instances of the same problem.
- Tasks involving tree and graph traversal.
- Recursive data structures like linked lists and binary trees.
- Mathematical problems like factorials and Fibonacci sequences.

**Iterative Approach:**

**Strengths:**

1. **Efficiency**: Iterative solutions can be more efficient in terms of time and space complexity, as they avoid the overhead of function calls.

2. **Predictable Space Usage**: Iteration typically uses a fixed amount of memory, making it more predictable in terms of space usage.

3. **Avoiding Stack Overflows**: Iterative approaches can be used in cases where stack overflow might be a concern with recursion.

**Weaknesses:**

1. **Code Repetition**: Iterative solutions may involve more code repetition compared to recursive solutions, which can affect code readability.

2. **Less Intuitive for Complex Structures**: Iteration might be less intuitive for problems involving complex structures like trees and graphs.

**When to Use Iteration:**

- Problems that can be efficiently solved using loops and iterations.

- Situations where performance and memory usage are critical.

- Tasks that don't naturally lend themselves to recursive breakdown.

**Choosing the Right Approach:**

- **Nature of the Problem**: Choose recursion when the problem can be naturally divided into smaller instances. Choose iteration when the problem is better suited for a loop-based approach.

- **Efficiency**: If performance and memory usage are crucial, consider iterative approaches for more predictable efficiency.

- **Complexity**: For problems involving complex structures or nested operations, recursion might provide a more elegant solution.

- **Stack Usage**: Be mindful of stack usage when using recursion, as excessive function calls can lead to stack overflow errors.

Recursive and iterative approaches are two distinct paths to problem-solving. While recursion offers elegant solutions by breaking problems into smaller parts, iteration focuses on efficiency and predictability. The choice between them depends on the problem's nature, the available resources, and the desired trade-offs between elegance and performance. By understanding the strengths and weaknesses of both approaches, you can navigate the landscape of algorithmic design and select the most appropriate method for the task at hand.

## Solving Problems with Recursion

Recursion is a powerful problem-solving technique that allows you to solve complex problems by breaking them down into smaller, similar subproblems. It's like solving a puzzle by solving smaller pieces, where each piece is a smaller instance of the same problem..

**Steps for Solving Problems with Recursion:**

1. **Identify Base Cases**: Start by identifying the simplest cases of the problem that can be solved directly without further recursion. These are the base cases that will stop the

recursion.

2. **Define Recursive Cases**: Determine how to break down the problem into smaller instances that resemble the original problem. This often involves calling the same function with modified parameters.

3. **Use Recursion**: Apply the recursive approach to solve the smaller instances of the problem. Recursively call the function to solve the subproblems.

4. **Combine Solutions**: Combine the solutions of the smaller instances to solve the original problem. This combination might involve mathematical operations, merging results, or applying logic.

**Recursive Problem-Solving in Action: Factorial Calculation**

A classic example of recursive problem-solving is calculating the factorial of a non-negative integer. The factorial of n (denoted as n!) is the product of all positive integers up to n.

```
def factorial(n):
    if n == 0:
        return 1
    else:
        return n * factorial(n - 1)
```

**Guidelines for Effective Recursive Solutions:**

1. **Keep It Simple**: Recursive solutions should focus on simplifying the problem, breaking it down into smaller components.

2. **Avoid Recalculation**: If a recursive solution involves repeated calculations, consider using memoization to store and reuse results.

3. **Careful Parameter Handling**: Ensure that the parameters passed to recursive calls are adjusted correctly to avoid infinite recursion.

4. **Use Helper Functions**: In some cases, using a helper function with additional parameters can make the recursive process smoother.

5. **Iterative Alternatives**: Sometimes, iterative solutions might be more efficient and easier to implement. Evaluate both approaches before making a choice.

**Real-World Applications of Recursive Problem-Solving:**

- Tree and graph traversal algorithms often use recursion to explore nodes and edges.

- Recursive problem-solving is applied in dynamic programming, a technique for solving optimization problems.

**Benefits of Recursive Problem-Solving:**

- **Elegance**: Recursive solutions often capture the essence of the problem's structure, leading to elegant and concise code.

- **Divide and Conquer**: Recursive thinking enables a divide-and-conquer strategy, breaking down complex problems into manageable pieces.

- **Problem Abstraction**: Recursion abstracts complex

problems into simpler subproblems, aiding understanding and solution design.

Recursion is a powerful approach that empowers you to tackle complex problems by breaking them into smaller instances of the same problem. By identifying base cases, defining recursive cases, and applying the recursive process, you can navigate intricate challenges more effectively. Recursive problem-solving is an essential skill for programmers, enabling you to create elegant, efficient, and elegant solutions across a wide range of domains and applications.

## Backtracking Algorithms

Backtracking is a problem-solving technique that involves exploring possible solutions by trying out different options and undoing them if they lead to dead ends. It's like navigating through a maze, where you backtrack to a previous point if you reach a dead end and explore a different path. Backtracking algorithms are particularly useful for solving problems that involve making a series of choices to find a viable solution.

**Principles of Backtracking:**

1. **Explore and Choose**: Backtracking involves exploring different choices or paths at each step to find a solution.

2. **Track Choices**: Maintain a record of choices made at each step, so you can undo them if needed.

3. **Backtrack on Failure**: If a chosen path leads to a dead

end, backtrack to a previous point and explore a different option.

4. **Base Case**: Define a base case that indicates when a solution is found or when backtracking should stop.

**Backtracking in Action: N-Queens Problem**

The N-Queens problem is a classic example of backtracking. Given an N×N chessboard, the task is to place N queens on the board such that no two queens threaten each other.

```python
def solve_n_queens(board, row):
    if row == len(board):
        # Base case: All queens are placed
        return True

    for col in range(len(board)):
        if is_safe(board, row, col):
            board[row][col] = 1  # Place queen
            if solve_n_queens(board, row + 1):
                return True  # Found a solution
            board[row][col] = 0  # Backtrack if no solution

    return False
```

**Applications of Backtracking:**

- **Puzzle Solving**: Backtracking is used in solving puzzles like Sudoku, N-Queens, and the Eight Puzzle.
- **Combinatorial Problems**: Problems involving combinations, permutations, and subsets can often be solved using backtracking.
- **Constraint Satisfaction**: Problems where you need to

satisfy certain constraints, like scheduling tasks, can be approached with backtracking.

- **Graph Problems**: Certain graph problems, like finding a Hamiltonian cycle, can be solved using backtracking.

## Steps for Implementing Backtracking:

1. **Choose**: Make a choice at the current step, marking it as part of the solution.
2. **Explore**: Recurse to explore the next step or level, making further choices.
3. **Constraint Check**: Check if the current choice violates any constraints. If it does, backtrack.
4. **Base Case**: Define a base case that indicates when a solution is found or when backtracking should stop.
5. **Backtrack**: If the current path doesn't lead to a solution, undo the last choice and try a different one.

## Benefits of Backtracking Algorithms:

- **Exploration**: Backtracking systematically explores possible solutions, ensuring no viable option is overlooked.
- **Optimization**: Backtracking can often lead to optimization by exploring only relevant paths.
- **Complex Problems**: Backtracking can handle complex problems with a large solution space.

## Challenges and Considerations:

- **Time Complexity**: In some cases, backtracking algorithms can have exponential time complexity.
- **Memory Usage**: Backtracking algorithms might require

significant memory for recording choices.

- **Efficiency**: Careful constraint-checking and pruning can improve the efficiency of backtracking.

Backtracking algorithms offer a systematic approach to solving complex problems by exploring different paths and choices. By understanding the principles of backtracking and how to apply them, you can develop solutions for puzzles, combinatorial problems, and constraint satisfaction tasks. While backtracking might be computationally expensive in some cases, its ability to explore solution spaces thoroughly makes it a valuable tool in the problem-solving toolkit of programmers and algorithm designers.

# CHAPTER 7: SEARCHING ALGORITHMS

Welcome to the captivating world of searching algorithms – the tools that allow you to find specific elements within a collection of data efficiently. In this chapter, we'll dive into various searching techniques, exploring how they work, their strengths, and how to choose the right one for different scenarios. Whether you're looking for a needle in a haystack or a specific piece of information in a dataset, searching algorithms are here to guide the way.

## Linear Search

Linear search, also known as sequential search, is a simple and straightforward searching algorithm that checks each element in a list or array one by one until it finds the target element or exhausts the entire list. While not the most efficient searching algorithm for large datasets, linear search is easy to understand and implement. It's like searching for a specific book in a library by going through each shelf until you find it.

**How Linear Search Works:**

1. **Start from the Beginning**: Begin the search from the first element of the list.

2. **Compare with Target**: Compare the current element with the target element you are searching for.

3. **Found or Not**: If the current element matches the target, the search is successful, and you can return the index of the element. If the end of the list is reached without a match, the element is not present.

**Linear Search in Python:**

Here's a basic implementation of linear search in Python:

```python
def linear_search(arr, target):
    for i in range(len(arr)):
        if arr[i] == target:
            return i  # Return the index of the target if found
    return -1  # Return -1 if target is not found
```

**Advantages and Disadvantages:**

**Advantages:**

- **Simplicity**: Linear search is easy to understand and implement, making it a good choice for small lists or when a more complex algorithm is unnecessary.

- **Unsorted Lists**: Linear search works well for unsorted lists, as it doesn't rely on any specific ordering.

**Disadvantages:**

- **Inefficient for Large Lists**: For large lists, linear search can be inefficient, as it needs to check each element one by one.

- **Time Complexity**: The worst-case time complexity of linear search is O(n), where n is the number of elements in the list.

**Real-World Applications:**

- Linear search is used when working with small datasets, where the overhead of more complex algorithms might not be justified.

- It's suitable for situations where the data is not sorted or when only a few searches need to be performed.

Linear search is a fundamental and straightforward searching algorithm that is easy to implement and understand. While it might not be the most efficient option for large datasets, it serves as a building block for learning about searching algorithms and can be useful in specific scenarios. By grasping the concept of linear search, you'll gain insights into the principles of searching and be better equipped to explore more advanced searching techniques.

## Binary Search: Principles and Implementation

Binary search is a powerful searching algorithm designed for efficiently locating a target element in a sorted list or array. Unlike linear search, which checks each element one by one, binary search reduces the search space by half with each comparison. It's like finding a word in a dictionary by opening the book in the middle and narrowing down your search based on alphabetical order.

**Principles of Binary Search:**

Binary search takes advantage of the sorted nature of the list to drastically reduce the search space. The algorithm compares the middle element of the current search interval to the target element. Depending on the comparison result, it then restricts the search to either the lower or upper half of the interval, effectively halving the possibilities with each iteration.

**Binary Search Implementation:**

Here's a step-by-step breakdown of how binary search works:

1. **Initialize Pointers**: Set two pointers, **left** and **right**, to the beginning and end of the list respectively.

2. **Calculate Middle**: Compute the middle index as **(left + right) // 2**.

3. **Compare and Adjust**: Compare the middle element with the target. If they are equal, return the middle index. If the middle element is greater than the target, adjust the **right** pointer to **mid - 1**. If the middle element is less than the target, adjust the **left** pointer to **mid + 1**.

4. **Repeat**: Repeat steps 2 and 3 until **left** is less than or equal to **right**.

5. **Exit**: If **left** is greater than **right** and the target is not found, return -1 to indicate that the target is not in the list.

**Binary Search Implementation in Python:**

```
def binary_search(arr, target):
    left, right = 0, len(arr) - 1
    while left <= right:
        mid = (left + right) // 2
        if arr[mid] == target:
            return mid  # Found target at index mid
        elif arr[mid] < target:
            left = mid + 1
        else:
            right = mid - 1
    return -1  # Target not found
```

**Advantages and Limitations:**

**Advantages:**

- **Efficiency**: Binary search is significantly more efficient than linear search, especially for large datasets.
- **Sorted Lists**: Binary search requires a sorted list, making it well-suited for scenarios where data is organized.

**Limitations:**

- **Sorted Requirement**: Binary search can only be applied to sorted lists. If the list is unsorted, a different search algorithm is necessary.
- **Memory Usage**: Binary search doesn't require additional memory, but its space complexity remains constant.

**Real-World Applications:**

- Binary search is used in various fields, such as databases, where quick access to sorted data is essential.
- It's commonly applied in computer science and programming to efficiently locate items in arrays.

Binary search is a highly efficient searching algorithm that takes advantage of sorted data to quickly locate a target element. By repeatedly halving the search space, binary search reduces the number of comparisons required to find the target. Understanding the principles of binary search and how to implement it allows you to efficiently search through sorted datasets, providing a valuable tool for problem-solving and information retrieval.

## Searching in Sorted and Rotated Arrays

Searching for an element in a sorted array is a common task, but what happens when the array is both sorted and rotated? In scenarios where the array has been rotated at an unknown pivot point, standard searching algorithms like binary search can still be applied with some modifications.

### The Challenge of Rotated Arrays:

In a rotated array, elements that were originally at the end can appear at the beginning after the rotation. This rotation disrupts the natural order, making standard binary search ineffective. However, the rotated array still preserves some order that can be leveraged for an efficient search.

### Searching in Rotated Arrays:

One approach to searching in rotated arrays involves applying a modified binary search. The idea is to divide the array into two halves and determine which half is sorted. Then, based on the sorted half and the target value, you can decide which portion of the array to focus on for the search.

**Steps for Searching in Rotated Arrays:**

1. **Find Midpoint**: Calculate the midpoint of the array (middle index).

2. **Check Sorted Half**: Compare the value at the midpoint with the value at the start of the array. If the midpoint value is greater, the left half is sorted. If the midpoint value is smaller, the right half is sorted.

3. **Check Target Range**: Check if the target value falls within the sorted half. If it does, perform a binary search within that half. If not, perform a search in the other half.

4. **Repeat**: Repeat steps 1-3 for the chosen half until the target is found or the search space is exhausted.

**Searching in Rotated Arrays in Python:**

Here's a Python implementation of the searching algorithm for rotated arrays:

```
def search_rotated_array(arr, target):
    left, right = 0, len(arr) - 1
    while left <= right:
        mid = (left + right) // 2
        if arr[mid] == target:
            return mid  # Found target at index mid

        if arr[left] <= arr[mid]:  # Left half is sorted
            if arr[left] <= target <= arr[mid]:
                right = mid - 1
            else:
                left = mid + 1
```

```
    else:  # Right half is sorted
      if arr[mid] <= target <= arr[right]:
        left = mid + 1
      else:
        right = mid - 1
  return -1  # Target not found
```

## Advantages and Limitations:

### Advantages:

- **Efficiency**: The search in rotated arrays maintains the efficiency of binary search, making it suitable for large datasets.

- **Versatility**: This technique works for both sorted and rotated arrays, providing a single solution for various scenarios.

### Limitations:

- **Sorted Requirement**: The algorithm assumes that the array is initially sorted before rotation.

- **Additional Checks**: The algorithm requires additional checks to determine the sorted half and the target's range.

### Real-World Applications:

- Searching in rotated arrays is applicable in scenarios where data is sorted and then rotated, such as in some encryption algorithms.

- It's also relevant in scenarios where the start and end of a cyclic pattern need to be determined.

Searching in sorted and rotated arrays introduces a new layer of complexity to traditional searching algorithms. By leveraging the partially sorted nature of rotated arrays, you can adapt binary search techniques to efficiently locate a target element. This approach demonstrates the adaptability of algorithms and the creativity required to solve unique problems. Understanding the principles of searching in rotated arrays equips you with a versatile skill that can be applied in scenarios where sorted data is subject to rotation.

## Hashing and Hash Tables

Hashing is a fundamental concept in computer science that provides an efficient way to store, retrieve, and manage data. At the core of hashing lies the concept of hash functions and hash tables, which allow for rapid data access and retrieval based on unique identifiers.

### Understanding Hashing:

Hashing involves transforming input data of arbitrary size into a fixed-size value, typically a numerical value or a hash code. This process is performed by a hash function, which converts the input data into a hash value.

### Hash Functions:

A hash function takes an input (often called a key) and maps it to a fixed-size value (the hash code). An ideal hash function should have the following properties:

1. **Deterministic**: For the same input, the hash function should always produce the same hash code.

2. **Fast Computation**: The hash function should be computationally efficient to calculate.

3. **Uniform Distribution**: Hash codes should be uniformly distributed to avoid clustering and collisions.

4. **Collision Resistance**: Collisions (different inputs producing the same hash code) should be minimized.

## Hash Tables:

A hash table is a data structure that uses hashing to store and retrieve values associated with keys. It consists of an array of buckets (also known as slots), where each bucket can hold one or more key-value pairs. The hash code generated by the hash function determines the index (bucket) where the data will be stored.

### Hash Table Operations:

1. **Insertion**: Insert a key-value pair into the hash table. The hash function is used to determine the index where the data will be stored.

2. **Retrieval**: Retrieve the value associated with a given key from the hash table. The hash function helps locate the appropriate bucket.

3. **Deletion**: Remove a key-value pair from the hash table.

## Collision Resolution:

Collisions occur when two different keys produce the same hash code, leading to the same index in the hash table. There are various techniques to handle collisions:

- **Separate Chaining**: Each bucket holds a linked list of key-value pairs, resolving collisions by chaining elements together.

- **Open Addressing**: When a collision occurs, the algorithm probes other locations in the hash table to find an empty slot.
- **Double Hashing**: A variation of open addressing where a second hash function determines the step size for probing.

## Hashing Applications:

- **Databases**: Hashing allows for quick data retrieval based on keys, making it ideal for indexing databases.
- **Caching**: Hashing can be used to quickly check if a value is already stored in a cache.
- **Cryptographic Applications**: Cryptographic hash functions are used for data integrity verification and password storage.

## Benefits of Hashing and Hash Tables:

- **Fast Retrieval**: Hashing provides rapid data access, allowing for constant-time retrieval in many cases.
- **Space Efficiency**: Hash tables can efficiently store and organize large amounts of data.
- **Versatility**: Hashing is used in a wide range of applications, from databases to security algorithms.

## Challenges and Considerations:

- **Collisions**: Handling collisions effectively is crucial for maintaining the efficiency of hash tables.
- **Choosing Hash Functions**: Selecting appropriate hash

functions for specific applications is important for uniform distribution.

Hashing and hash tables are essential tools for efficient data management and retrieval. By leveraging hash functions and organizing data into buckets, hash tables provide rapid access to information based on keys. The versatility of hashing makes it a foundational concept in computer science, with applications spanning databases, caching, security, and more. Understanding how to design and use hash functions and hash tables equips you with the ability to handle data efficiently and solve various real-world challenges.

# CHAPTER 8: SORTING ALGORITHMS

Welcome to the world of sorting algorithms, where the art of arranging elements in a specific order comes to life. Sorting is a fundamental operation in computer science, and understanding various sorting techniques is essential for optimizing data manipulation tasks. In this chapter, we'll embark on a journey through different sorting algorithms, exploring their principles, strengths, and when to choose one over the other. Whether you're organizing a list of names or optimizing the performance of your application, sorting algorithms are the key to order and efficiency.

## Importance of Sorting

Sorting is a fundamental operation in computer science with widespread significance across various domains. It plays a crucial role in data organization, search optimization, and data analysis. Understanding the importance of sorting helps us appreciate its impact on efficiency, user experiences, and problem-solving.

## Data Organization and Retrieval:

One of the primary reasons for sorting is to organize data in a meaningful order. Imagine a library without any organized arrangement of books—it would be challenging to find the book you're looking for. Similarly, in computer applications, sorting ensures that data is structured in a way that facilitates efficient retrieval. This organization becomes especially valuable as datasets grow larger.

## Search Optimization:

Sorted data allows for optimized search operations. In a sorted list, you can use techniques like binary search to quickly locate specific elements. Binary search reduces the search space by half with each comparison, making it significantly faster than linear search for larger datasets. Sorting thus transforms the search process from a linear time complexity to a logarithmic time complexity, resulting in a substantial speedup.

## User Experiences:

Sorting directly impacts user experiences in applications. Imagine an e-commerce website where products are displayed in a random order. It would be challenging for users to find what they're looking for, leading to frustration and reduced user engagement. On the other hand, presenting products in a sorted order—perhaps based on relevance, price, or popularity—enhances usability and encourages users to explore more.

## Data Analysis and Insights:

In data analysis, sorting is often a preliminary step to gain insights from raw data. Sorting data based on specific criteria allows you to identify trends, outliers, and patterns more effectively. This organized view of data forms the foundation for various analytical techniques, helping you make informed decisions and draw meaningful conclusions.

**Efficient Algorithms:**

Many algorithms and data structures rely on sorted data to achieve efficiency. For example, balanced binary search trees (such as AVL trees and Red-Black trees) maintain data in a sorted order to ensure quick operations like insertion, deletion, and search. Sorting enables these structures to maintain balance and optimize their performance.

**Real-World Applications:**

- **Databases**: Sorting accelerates database query performance by allowing efficient indexing and data retrieval.
- **Search Engines**: Search engines sort search results based on relevance to enhance user experience.
- **Financial Analysis**: Sorting financial data aids in identifying trends and making investment decisions.
- **Logistics**: Sorting packages for delivery routes improves logistics efficiency.

The importance of sorting transcends mere data arrangement; it impacts efficiency, user experiences, and decision-making across diverse applications. Sorting empowers us to navigate through data with ease, optimize search operations, and extract valuable insights. Whether it's making applications user-friendly, analyzing large datasets, or implementing efficient algorithms, sorting stands as a cornerstone of computer science, shaping the way we interact with and understand data.

## Bubble Sort and Selection Sort: Simple Sorting Algorithms

Bubble Sort and Selection Sort are basic sorting algorithms that provide a foundational understanding of sorting principles. While not the most efficient options for large datasets, these algorithms introduce the concept of sorting by repeatedly comparing and rearranging elements.

**Bubble Sort:**

Bubble Sort is a straightforward sorting algorithm that repeatedly steps through a list, compares adjacent elements, and swaps them if they are in the wrong order. The process is similar to repeatedly bubbling the largest element to the end of the list. Although Bubble Sort is relatively simple, it's not the most efficient choice for large datasets due to its quadratic time complexity.

**Bubble Sort Steps:**

1. Start from the beginning of the list.
2. Compare adjacent elements. If they are in the wrong order, swap them.
3. Continue the process for each element until the entire list is sorted.

## Bubble Sort Implementation in Python:

```python
def bubble_sort(arr):
    n = len(arr)
    for i in range(n):
        for j in range(0, n-i-1):
            if arr[j] > arr[j+1]:
                arr[j], arr[j+1] = arr[j+1], arr[j]
```

## Selection Sort:

Selection Sort is another simple sorting algorithm that divides the list into two parts: a sorted portion and an unsorted portion. It repeatedly selects the smallest (or largest, depending on the sorting order) element from the unsorted portion and places it at the end of the sorted portion. Similar to Bubble Sort, Selection Sort is easy to understand but not the most efficient for larger datasets.

### Selection Sort Steps:

1. Find the minimum (or maximum) element in the unsorted portion.
2. Swap it with the first element of the unsorted portion.
3. Expand the sorted portion by one element and repeat the process.

### Selection Sort Implementation in Python:

```python
def selection_sort(arr):
    n = len(arr)
    for i in range(n):
        min_index = i
        for j in range(i+1, n):
```

```
if arr[j] < arr[min_index]:
    min_index = j
arr[i], arr[min_index] = arr[min_index], arr[i]
```

## Advantages and Limitations:

### Advantages:

- Both Bubble Sort and Selection Sort are easy to understand and implement, making them suitable for educational purposes and small datasets.

### Limitations:

- Quadratic Time Complexity: Bubble Sort and Selection Sort have quadratic time complexity (O(n^2)), which makes them inefficient for large datasets.
- Not Suitable for Large Data: These algorithms become slow as the number of elements increases, making them unsuitable for practical use with substantial datasets.

### Real-World Applications:

- Due to their simplicity, Bubble Sort and Selection Sort are often used in educational contexts to introduce sorting concepts to beginners.
- They can be useful for small datasets or situations where performance is not a primary concern.

Bubble Sort and Selection Sort serve as introductory examples of sorting algorithms, helping beginners grasp the core concepts of sorting and comparisons. While they are not the most efficient options for larger datasets, understanding these algorithms lays the foundation for exploring more advanced sorting techniques. These algorithms showcase the essence of sorting: comparing and arranging elements to achieve a desired order, whether for educational purposes or in small-scale scenarios.

## Insertion Sort and Shell Sort: Building Blocks of Sorting

Insertion Sort and Shell Sort are sorting algorithms that offer efficiency improvements over Bubble Sort and Selection Sort for small datasets. Insertion Sort, in particular, is well-suited for partially sorted or nearly sorted lists, making it a valuable tool in certain scenarios. Shell Sort builds upon the principles of Insertion Sort and introduces the concept of gap sequences to improve efficiency.

**Insertion Sort:**

Insertion Sort is a simple sorting algorithm that builds a sorted list by gradually inserting elements from the unsorted portion into the sorted portion. It's similar to sorting a hand of cards by repeatedly inserting a card into its correct position among the already sorted cards. Insertion Sort is efficient for small datasets or partially sorted lists.

**Insertion Sort Steps:**

1. Start with the second element (index 1) and consider it as the key.
2. Compare the key with the previous elements in the sorted portion, moving larger elements one position ahead.

3. Insert the key into its correct position within the sorted portion.

4. Repeat steps 2 and 3 for each element in the unsorted portion.

**Insertion Sort Implementation in Python:**

```python
def insertion_sort(arr):
    for i in range(1, len(arr)):
        key = arr[i]
        j = i - 1
        while j >= 0 and key < arr[j]:
            arr[j + 1] = arr[j]
            j -= 1
        arr[j + 1] = key
```

**Shell Sort:**

Shell Sort is an extension of Insertion Sort that introduces the concept of gap sequences. The algorithm divides the list into smaller sublists and sorts each sublist using Insertion Sort. As the algorithm progresses, the sublists become smaller and the list becomes more sorted. The choice of gap sequence affects the efficiency of Shell Sort.

**Shell Sort Steps:**

1. Choose a gap sequence (e.g., Knuth's sequence: 1, 4, 13, ...).

2. Divide the list into sublists of the chosen gap size.

3. Sort each sublist using Insertion Sort.

4. Reduce the gap size and repeat steps 2 and 3.

5. Continue until the gap size becomes 1, effectively performing a final Insertion Sort.

**Shell Sort Implementation in Python:**

```python
def shell_sort(arr):
    n = len(arr)
    gap = n // 2
    while gap > 0:
        for i in range(gap, n):
            temp = arr[i]
            j = i
            while j >= gap and arr[j - gap] > temp:
                arr[j] = arr[j - gap]
                j -= gap
            arr[j] = temp
        gap //= 2
```

**Advantages and Limitations:**

**Advantages:**

- Both Insertion Sort and Shell Sort are efficient for small datasets or partially sorted lists.

- Insertion Sort performs well on nearly sorted lists.

**Limitations:**

- Quadratic Time Complexity: While better than Bubble Sort and Selection Sort, Insertion Sort and Shell Sort still have quadratic time complexity ($O(n^2)$), making them inefficient for large datasets.

**Real-World Applications:**

- Insertion Sort is useful when you know that the list is

almost sorted, as it has a small number of comparisons and swaps.

- Shell Sort is used when you want to sort elements in larger steps first to partially sort the list and then refine it further.

Insertion Sort and Shell Sort provide intermediate steps between basic sorting algorithms and more advanced techniques like Merge Sort and Quick Sort. These algorithms offer efficiency improvements over their predecessors, making them valuable for certain scenarios. Insertion Sort's simplicity and adaptability to nearly sorted lists make it handy, while Shell Sort's introduction of gap sequences adds a layer of optimization. By understanding these algorithms, you gain insights into sorting strategies that bridge the gap between basic and advanced sorting techniques.

## Merge Sort: Divide and Conquer for Efficient Sorting

Merge Sort is a highly efficient sorting algorithm that employs the "divide and conquer" strategy to sort elements. By breaking down the sorting process into smaller subproblems and then merging the sorted solutions, Merge Sort achieves superior time complexity compared to earlier algorithms.

### Divide and Conquer Strategy:

Merge Sort follows the "divide and conquer" paradigm, which involves breaking down a problem into smaller, more manageable subproblems. These subproblems are solved independently and then combined to form the solution to the original problem. For sorting, Merge Sort divides the array into smaller subarrays, sorts them, and then merges them to create a fully sorted array.

**Merge Sort Steps:**

1. **Divide**: Divide the unsorted array into two equal halves.
2. **Conquer**: Recursively sort each half.
3. **Merge**: Merge the sorted halves to create a single sorted array.

**Merge Sort Implementation in Python:**

```python
def merge_sort(arr):
    if len(arr) <= 1:
        return arr

    mid = len(arr) // 2
    left_half = merge_sort(arr[:mid])
    right_half = merge_sort(arr[mid:])

    return merge(left_half, right_half)

def merge(left, right):
    result = []
    left_idx, right_idx = 0, 0

    while left_idx < len(left) and right_idx < len(right):
        if left[left_idx] < right[right_idx]:
            result.append(left[left_idx])
            left_idx += 1
        else:
            result.append(right[right_idx])
            right_idx += 1

    result.extend(left[left_idx:])
    result.extend(right[right_idx:])
```

```
return result
```

**Advantages of Merge Sort:**

1. **Efficient Time Complexity**: Merge Sort guarantees a worst-case time complexity of O(n log n), making it suitable for sorting large datasets.

2. **Stable Sorting**: Merge Sort is stable, meaning that the relative order of equal elements remains preserved after sorting.

3. **Suitable for External Sorting**: Merge Sort's efficient use of external memory makes it useful for sorting large datasets that do not fit into main memory.

**Real-World Applications:**

- **External Sorting**: Merge Sort's ability to handle large datasets with external memory makes it valuable for sorting data stored on external storage devices.

- **File Merging**: Merge Sort is often used in external sorting scenarios like merging multiple sorted files.

- **Parallel Processing**: Merge Sort can be parallelized to take advantage of multi-core processors, further enhancing its performance.

Merge Sort is a versatile and efficient sorting algorithm that uses the divide and conquer strategy to provide a predictable and fast sorting solution. By breaking down the sorting process into smaller parts and merging the results, Merge Sort achieves a balanced trade-off between time complexity and memory usage. Understanding the principles of Merge Sort equips you with a powerful tool for efficiently handling sorting tasks, particularly for large datasets or scenarios with external memory constraints.

## Quick Sort: Pivot and Partition for Swift Sorting

Quick Sort is a highly efficient sorting algorithm that utilizes the "divide and conquer" strategy, similar to Merge Sort. However, Quick Sort takes a different approach by choosing a pivot element and partitioning the array into two segments: elements less than the pivot and elements greater than the pivot. This process continues recursively until the entire array is sorted.

**Divide and Conquer Strategy:**

Like Merge Sort, Quick Sort follows the "divide and conquer" strategy. It divides the array into smaller subarrays, sorts them, and then combines the sorted subarrays to obtain a fully sorted array. The key difference lies in the choice of pivot element and the partitioning process.

**Quick Sort Steps:**

1. **Choose Pivot**: Select a pivot element from the array.
2. **Partitioning**: Partition the array into two segments: elements less than the pivot and elements greater than the pivot.
3. **Recursively Sort**: Recursively sort both segments.
4. **Combine**: Combine the sorted segments to obtain the fully

sorted array.

**Quick Sort Implementation in Python:**

```python
def quick_sort(arr):
    if len(arr) <= 1:
        return arr

    pivot = arr[len(arr) // 2]
    left = [x for x in arr if x < pivot]
    middle = [x for x in arr if x == pivot]
    right = [x for x in arr if x > pivot]

    return quick_sort(left) + middle + quick_sort(right)
```

**Advantages of Quick Sort:**

1. **Efficient Time Complexity**: Quick Sort has an average-case time complexity of O(n log n), making it one of the fastest sorting algorithms in practice.

2. **In-Place Sorting**: Quick Sort can be implemented in-place, meaning it doesn't require additional memory for sorting.

3. **Adaptable to Data Distribution**: Quick Sort performs well even when the data is not uniformly distributed.

**Real-World Applications:**

- **Standard Library Sorting**: Many programming languages and libraries use Quick Sort as their default sorting algorithm due to its efficiency.

- **Array Sorting**: Quick Sort is commonly used to sort arrays in various applications, including database systems.

- **Data Analysis**: Quick Sort's fast average-case performance makes it suitable for sorting data during analysis and calculations.

**Pivot Selection and Partitioning:**

The choice of pivot element significantly influences Quick Sort's performance. An ideal pivot divides the array into roughly equal segments, minimizing the number of recursive calls. Strategies for pivot selection include choosing the first element, the last element, the middle element, or a random element. Each strategy has its trade-offs, and some implementations even use median-of-three or median-of-five strategies for better pivot selection.

**Partitioning** is the process of rearranging the elements so that elements less than the pivot are on its left and elements greater than the pivot are on its right. This step is crucial for Quick Sort's efficiency. One common partitioning technique is the Hoare partition scheme, which uses two pointers that move toward each other to swap elements.

Quick Sort's pivot and partition approach provides a swift and efficient method for sorting arrays. By dividing the array based on a pivot element and then partitioning it into smaller segments, Quick Sort achieves fast average-case performance. Its in-place nature and adaptability to various data distributions make it a popular choice for sorting tasks across different applications. Understanding Quick Sort's pivot selection and partitioning process equips you with a powerful sorting tool that balances efficiency and memory usage.

## Comparing Sorting Algorithms: Making Informed Choices

Sorting algorithms come in a variety of flavors, each with its own strengths, weaknesses, and trade-offs. Choosing the right sorting algorithm for a particular task depends on factors such as the size of the dataset, the distribution of data, memory constraints, and desired time complexity.

**Performance Metrics:**

When comparing sorting algorithms, several performance metrics help evaluate their efficiency:

1. **Time Complexity**: Describes how the execution time of an algorithm grows with the size of the input data. Algorithms with lower time complexity are generally more efficient.

2. **Space Complexity**: Refers to the memory space required by an algorithm to execute. Algorithms that use less memory are preferred, especially in resource-constrained environments.

3. **Stability**: A stable sorting algorithm preserves the relative order of equal elements. Stability matters when maintaining the order of data with multiple keys.

4. **Adaptability**: Some algorithms perform better on partially sorted data. An adaptive algorithm's efficiency improves in such scenarios.

**Comparing Algorithms:**

**Bubble Sort and Selection Sort**: These algorithms are simple to understand but have quadratic time complexity ($O(n^2)$), making them inefficient for large datasets. They are suitable for educational purposes or small datasets.

**Insertion Sort**: Efficient for small datasets or partially sorted data. It has quadratic time complexity ($O(n^2)$) but performs well on nearly sorted lists.

**Merge Sort**: Guarantees $O(n \log n)$ time complexity and is stable. Its external memory use makes it useful for large datasets that don't fit in main memory.

**Quick Sort**: Offers fast average-case performance ($O(n \log n)$) and is suitable for most scenarios. It's efficient, in-place variants exist, and it's used as a default sorting algorithm in many libraries.

**Shell Sort**: Performs better than quadratic time complexity for medium-sized datasets. Its choice of gap sequence affects efficiency.

**Choosing the Right Algorithm:**

1. **Input Size**: For small datasets, simple algorithms like Bubble Sort, Selection Sort, or Insertion Sort may suffice. For larger datasets, algorithms with lower time complexity like Merge Sort, Quick Sort, or Shell Sort are preferred.

2. **Data Characteristics**: Algorithms behave differently based on data distribution. Quick Sort is adaptive to various data distributions, while Merge Sort maintains stability.

3. **Memory Constraints**: If memory usage is a concern, consider in-place sorting algorithms like Quick Sort or

Heap Sort.

4. **Stability**: If preserving the order of equal elements matters, opt for stable sorting algorithms like Merge Sort or Insertion Sort.

5. **Real-World Constraints**: Consider the specific context in which sorting is performed. External memory, parallel processing, and available libraries may influence your choice.

**Comparing in Practice:**

In real-world scenarios, it's essential to test sorting algorithms on representative datasets. Profiling tools help measure actual execution times and memory usage, allowing you to make an informed choice based on your application's requirements.

Comparing sorting algorithms involves a balance between time complexity, space complexity, stability, and adaptability. The choice of algorithm depends on the size and nature of the data, as well as any memory or performance constraints. Understanding the trade-offs and strengths of different sorting algorithms empowers you to select the most suitable one for your specific task, optimizing performance and achieving efficient data manipulation.

# CHAPTER 9: HASHING AND DICTIONARIES

Welcome to the world of efficient data retrieval and storage through hashing and dictionaries. In this chapter, we'll dive into the concepts of hashing, hash functions, and dictionaries—powerful tools for organizing, searching, and managing data. Whether you're building a database, implementing a cache, or optimizing data access, understanding hashing and dictionaries is essential. Let's explore how these concepts work and their real-world applications.

## Understanding Hashing: Efficient Data Transformation

Hashing is a versatile technique that plays a pivotal role in computer science and data management. It's the process of converting input data of arbitrary size into a fixed-size value, often referred to as a hash code or hash value. Hashing facilitates efficient data retrieval, storage, and verification.

### The Essence of Hashing:

Imagine you have a collection of items, each associated with a unique key. Hashing provides a way to transform these keys into indices within a fixed-size array. This enables rapid data access by eliminating the need to search linearly through the entire collection.

### Hash Functions: Mapping Keys to Indices:

At the heart of hashing lies the hash function. A hash function takes an input (the key) and produces a hash code—a numerical value that corresponds to an index in the hash table. Hash functions ensure that keys are transformed into indices uniformly and deterministically. This means that the same key will always generate the same hash code, making data retrieval consistent.

### Desirable Properties of Hash Functions:

- **Deterministic**: Given the same input, a hash function produces the same hash code every time.
- **Uniform Distribution**: Hash function outputs should be evenly distributed across the range of hash codes to minimize collisions (multiple keys producing the same hash code).
- **Efficiency**: Hash functions should be computationally efficient to avoid slowing down data operations.

### Applications of Hashing:

**Data Retrieval**: Hashing is widely used in databases, where keys (such as IDs) are hashed to quickly retrieve corresponding records.

**Caching**: In caching systems, hash codes determine whether requested data is present in the cache, preventing the need to access slower storage.

**Cryptographic Hashing**: Hash functions play a crucial role in cryptography, securing passwords and verifying data integrity.

**Distributed Systems**: Hashing helps distribute data evenly across multiple servers, ensuring efficient load balancing.

### Real-World Analogy: The Phone Book Example:

Consider a phone book where people are listed alphabetically by their last names. To find someone's phone number, you'd navigate directly to the section that corresponds to the initial letter of their last name. This is similar to how hashing maps keys to indices—providing swift access without the need to scan the entire list.

### Challenges and Considerations:

**Collisions**: Collisions occur when different keys produce the same hash code. Hash functions and collision resolution techniques (like separate chaining or open addressing) address this challenge.

**Choosing Hash Functions**: Selecting a suitable hash function is critical. A poor choice can lead to uneven distribution and reduced efficiency.

Hashing is a cornerstone of modern computing, providing an efficient way to manage and access data. Through the magic of hash functions, input data is transformed into compact representations that enable swift data retrieval and storage.

Understanding the essence of hashing empowers you to build optimized data structures, design secure systems, and harness the power of efficient data manipulation.

## Hash Maps and Dictionaries: Organizing Key-Value Pairs

Hash maps and dictionaries are essential data structures that utilize hashing to efficiently store and retrieve key-value pairs. These structures provide a powerful way to manage and manipulate data, offering rapid access and storage capabilities.

**Hash Maps and Dictionaries:**

A hash map (also known as a hash table) and a dictionary are interchangeable terms that refer to a data structure designed to hold key-value pairs. Each key is associated with a value, creating a mapping between the two.

**Hashing for Key Indexing:**

The magic of hash maps lies in their ability to use keys as input to a hash function, producing hash codes that directly correspond to indices within the underlying array. This enables quick retrieval and storage of values based on their associated keys.

**Operations on Hash Maps and Dictionaries:**

1. **Insertion**: Add a new key-value pair to the hash map.
2. **Retrieval**: Retrieve the value associated with a specific key.
3. **Deletion**: Remove a key-value pair from the hash map.

**Collision Handling:**

Collisions occur when two distinct keys produce the same hash code. Various techniques exist to manage collisions:

- **Separate Chaining**: Each bucket of the hash map holds a linked list of key-value pairs.
- **Open Addressing**: Colliding elements are stored in nearby empty slots within the array.
- **Double Hashing**: A secondary hash function is used to determine the next available slot when a collision occurs.

**Advantages of Hash Maps and Dictionaries:**

- **Rapid Access**: Hash maps offer constant-time (O(1)) access to values, making them ideal for situations where fast data retrieval is crucial.
- **Dynamic Sizing**: Hash maps can dynamically resize to accommodate more data, adapting to changing requirements.
- **Efficient Storage**: Hash maps use memory efficiently, as they allocate space only for the actual data stored.

**Dictionaries in Python:**

Python's built-in **dict** data structure is a widely used dictionary implementation. It leverages hashing to provide fast key-based data manipulation.

**Real-World Applications:**

- **Databases**: Hash maps speed up data retrieval in databases by quickly locating records based on their keys.
- **Caching**: Hash maps are used in caching systems to determine if requested data is present in the cache.

- **Language Translations**: Dictionaries are used for language translation, where each word corresponds to its translation.

- **Configuration Settings**: Hash maps store configuration settings, where keys represent options and values represent settings.

**Choosing Hash Maps and Dictionaries:**

When selecting a hash map or dictionary implementation, consider factors like:

- **Collision Handling Strategy**: Different strategies suit different scenarios; choose one that aligns with your needs.

- **Memory Efficiency**: Hash maps optimize memory usage by only storing actual data.

- **Time Complexity**: Hash maps offer fast retrieval, but it's essential to understand the average and worst-case scenarios.

Hash maps and dictionaries provide efficient ways to manage key-value pairs, offering quick data access and storage capabilities. By leveraging hashing techniques, these structures optimize data manipulation tasks in various applications, from databases to caching systems. Understanding how hash maps and dictionaries work equips you with a powerful tool for organizing and retrieving data, contributing to efficient and well-structured software systems.

# Collision Resolution Techniques: Tackling Hashing Conflicts

Collision resolution techniques are essential in hashing when two different keys produce the same hash code, resulting in a collision. Handling collisions effectively is crucial to ensure the integrity and efficiency of hash maps, dictionaries, and other hash-based data structures.

**The Collision Problem:**

Collisions occur when multiple keys generate the same hash code, leading to ambiguity in determining the correct index for data storage. Handling collisions ensures that data can be stored and retrieved accurately despite hash code conflicts.

**1. Separate Chaining:**

Separate chaining involves placing all colliding elements into the same bucket using a linked list. Each bucket contains a list of key-value pairs. When a collision happens, the new key-value pair is simply appended to the linked list of the corresponding bucket.

**Advantages**:

- Simple to implement.
- Suitable for scenarios where the number of collisions is expected to be low.

**Drawbacks**:

- Increased memory usage due to storing pointers for linked lists.
- Degraded performance if a bucket's linked list becomes too long.

## 2. Open Addressing:

Open addressing requires placing colliding elements within the array itself, in nearby empty slots. When a collision occurs, the algorithm probes for the next available slot, following a predetermined sequence (like linear probing or quadratic probing).

**Advantages**:

- No additional memory overhead for linked lists.
- Suitable for scenarios with minimal collisions.

**Drawbacks**:

- Clustering: Collisions can lead to clusters of occupied slots, causing further collisions.
- Performance degradation as the array fills up.

## 3. Double Hashing:

Double hashing combines the concepts of open addressing and multiple hash functions. When a collision occurs, a secondary hash function is applied to determine the next slot to probe. The secondary hash function should produce different results for different keys.

**Advantages**:

- Helps avoid clustering caused by linear or quadratic probing.
- Can offer better distribution and reduced collisions with a well-chosen secondary hash function.

**Drawbacks**:

- More complex implementation compared to basic open addressing.

## Choosing the Right Technique:

- **Separate Chaining**: Suitable for scenarios with a higher likelihood of collisions or when memory usage is less of a concern.

- **Open Addressing**: Preferable when memory usage needs to be minimized and the dataset is relatively small.

- **Double Hashing**: Effective when the potential for clustering is a concern and a suitable secondary hash function is available.

## Performance Considerations:

The choice of collision resolution technique significantly impacts the performance of hash-based data structures. Factors to consider include the expected number of collisions, memory constraints, and the distribution of the hash function.

Collision resolution techniques are crucial for maintaining the efficiency and reliability of hash-based data structures. Whether using separate chaining, open addressing, or double hashing, the goal is to ensure that keys are stored and retrieved accurately even when collisions occur. By understanding and selecting the appropriate collision resolution technique, you can create hash-based data structures that efficiently manage data and provide quick access to stored information.

# Hash Sets and Their Applications: Efficient Set Operations

Hash sets are data structures that leverage the power of hashing to store a collection of distinct elements. These structures provide rapid membership testing and efficient set operations, making them invaluable for various applications.

### Hash Sets: A Distinctive Collection:

A hash set is a collection of elements, similar to a mathematical set, but with the added benefits of fast data retrieval and manipulation. Hash sets ensure that each element is unique—no duplicates are allowed.

### Efficient Set Operations:

Hash sets excel in set operations such as insertion, deletion, and membership testing. These operations have a constant-time average complexity (O(1)), making hash sets ideal for scenarios where quick access to data is crucial.

### Hashing for Membership Testing:

To check if an element is present in a hash set, the hash set applies the same hash function to the element's value. The resulting hash code points to an index in the underlying array, where the element should be found if it exists.

### Advantages of Hash Sets:

- **Rapid Membership Testing**: Hash sets offer instantaneous confirmation of an element's presence or absence.
- **Efficient Insertion and Deletion**: Hash sets allow for quick addition and removal of elements.

- **Distinct Element Storage**: Hash sets ensure that each element is unique.

**Applications of Hash Sets:**

**Removing Duplicates**: Hash sets are used to remove duplicate entries from a list, ensuring that only distinct elements remain.

**Searching for Common Elements**: Hash sets help identify common elements between multiple lists, arrays, or datasets.

**Caching**: Hash sets can be employed in caching systems to store recently accessed items, ensuring efficient caching operations.

**Word Frequency Counting**: Hash sets assist in counting the frequency of words in a text by tracking unique words encountered.

**Real-World Analogy: The Guest List Example:**

Imagine hosting a party and maintaining a list of invited guests. A hash set would be like having a quick way to check if a particular person is on the guest list. Instead of scanning through the entire list, you can immediately verify their presence by checking the hash set.

**Choosing Hash Sets:**

When selecting a hash set implementation, consider:

- **Load Factor**: The ratio of occupied slots to the total number of slots. A higher load factor may lead to more collisions and degraded performance.
- **Hash Function**: The quality of the hash function affects distribution and efficiency.

Hash sets are powerful tools for efficiently managing collections of distinct elements. By leveraging hashing techniques, hash sets provide swift membership testing and set operations, improving data manipulation tasks in various applications. Understanding the advantages and applications of hash sets equips you with a versatile data structure that enhances your ability to efficiently handle and process data collections.

# CHAPTER 10: TREES AND BINARY TREES

Welcome to the captivating world of trees—a fundamental data structure that shapes the foundation of hierarchical organization and efficient data manipulation. In this chapter, we'll embark on a journey through trees and their various forms, focusing particularly on binary trees. By understanding the concepts of trees and binary trees, you'll gain insights into their structure, traversal methods, and real-world applications.

## Introduction to Trees and Hierarchical Structures

Welcome to the captivating realm of trees—a fundamental data structure that mirrors hierarchical relationships in the real world. Trees are vital tools for organizing, navigating, and managing data in a structured manner.

### The Concept of Trees:

Imagine a tree—the majestic structure with roots, a trunk, branches, and leaves. Just as a real tree has a hierarchical structure, data trees in computer science exhibit a similar arrangement. A tree consists of nodes connected by edges, forming a branching structure that flows from a root to various levels of branches.

**Tree Terminology:**

- **Node**: The basic building block of a tree, containing data and possibly linked to child nodes.
- **Root**: The topmost node that serves as the starting point of the tree's hierarchy.
- **Parent**: A node directly above another node in the hierarchy.
- **Child**: A node directly below another node in the hierarchy.
- **Leaf**: A node with no children—the end point of a branch.
- **Edge**: The connection between two nodes in a tree.

**Hierarchical Relationships and Trees:**

Trees model hierarchical relationships prevalent in many aspects of life. Consider a family tree, where each person represents a node, and parent-child relationships form the branches. Similarly, a directory structure in a computer's file system is a tree, with folders representing nodes and their nested contents forming the hierarchy.

**Key Features of Trees:**

1. **Hierarchy**: Trees follow a hierarchical structure, with a clear top-to-bottom organization.
2. **Uniqueness**: Each node has a unique parent, except for the root.

3. **No Cycles**: Unlike graphs, trees do not contain cycles (loops).

**Types of Trees:**

- **Binary Trees**: Each node has at most two children—left and right.
- **N-ary Trees**: Nodes can have more than two children.
- **Binary Search Trees (BST)**: A binary tree with a specific ordering property (left child is smaller, right child is larger).

**Real-World Analogies:**

Think of a company's organizational structure—a hierarchy of employees, managers, and executives. This structure can be modeled as a tree, with each employee representing a node, and the hierarchy forming the branches.

Trees provide a natural and powerful way to organize and represent hierarchical relationships in various domains. From family trees to file systems, trees are versatile structures that enable efficient data management and navigation. By grasping the fundamental concepts of trees and their terminology, you'll be equipped to explore the depths of tree-based data structures and algorithms, enhancing your ability to design and implement well-organized software systems.

## Binary Trees: Concepts and Properties

Binary trees are a foundational data structure in computer

science, known for their elegant and efficient hierarchical organization.

**Understanding Binary Trees:**

A binary tree is a tree structure in which each node can have at most two children—a left child and a right child. This unique arrangement creates a natural branching pattern that enables efficient data manipulation and traversal.

**Binary Tree Terminology:**

- **Root**: The topmost node in a binary tree from which all other nodes descend.
- **Parent**: A node directly above another node in the hierarchy.
- **Child**: A node directly below another node in the hierarchy.
- **Leaf**: A node with no children—a terminal point in the hierarchy.
- **Internal Node**: A node with at least one child.
- **Subtree**: A portion of a binary tree that comprises a node and its descendants.

**Properties of Binary Trees:**

1. **Depth and Height**: The depth of a node is the number of edges from the root to that node. The height of a tree is the maximum depth of any node.

2. **Balanced Binary Trees**: A balanced binary tree is one in which the height of the left and right subtrees of any node differs by at most one. Balanced trees ensure efficient

operations.

3. **Full Binary Trees**: In a full binary tree, every node has either zero or two children. All levels are completely filled.

4. **Complete Binary Trees**: A complete binary tree is a tree in which all levels are completely filled, except possibly the last level, which is filled from left to right.

5. **Perfect Binary Trees**: A perfect binary tree is a full binary tree where all internal nodes have exactly two children, and all leaf nodes are at the same level.

**Binary Tree Classification:**

Binary trees can be classified based on the number of children a node can have:

- **Strict Binary Tree**: Each node has either zero or two children.

- **Complete Binary Tree**: Every level is completely filled, except possibly the last, which is filled from left to right.

- **Degenerate (or Skewed) Tree**: A tree where each parent node has only one child, leading to a tree that is essentially a linked list.

**Real-World Applications:**

- **Expression Parsing**: Binary trees are used to parse and evaluate mathematical expressions.

- **File Systems**: Hierarchical file systems are often organized as binary trees.

- **Database Indexing**: Binary trees speed up data retrieval in databases through indexing.

- **Game Development**: Binary trees model game states and decision trees in games.

Binary trees are fundamental structures that offer a streamlined way to organize hierarchical data. Their versatile nature and efficient traversal methods make them invaluable in various applications, from parsing expressions to managing file systems. By understanding the concepts and properties of binary trees, you'll be equipped to design and implement efficient algorithms, optimize data storage, and explore more advanced tree-based structures and algorithms.

## Binary Tree Traversal: Inorder, Preorder, Postorder

Binary tree traversal is a fundamental technique that enables you to visit all nodes of a binary tree in a specific order. The three primary traversal methods—Inorder, Preorder, and Postorder—each offer unique insights into the tree's structure and are crucial for a variety of algorithms and applications.

### Inorder Traversal:

In an Inorder traversal, you start from the root and traverse the tree by visiting the left subtree first, then the root, and finally the right subtree. In other words, you visit nodes in the order of (left, root, right).

### Applications of Inorder Traversal:

- **Binary Search Trees**: Inorder traversal of a binary search tree yields nodes in ascending order.

- **Expression Evaluation**: In an expression tree, Inorder traversal retrieves the original expression.
- **Data Extraction**: Inorder traversal is used to extract data from binary trees for further processing.

**Preorder Traversal:**

In a Preorder traversal, you start from the root and traverse the tree by visiting the root first, then the left subtree, and finally the right subtree. The order is (root, left, right).

**Applications of Preorder Traversal:**

- **Expression Parsing**: Preorder traversal helps reconstruct the original expression from an expression tree.
- **Copying Trees**: Preorder traversal is used to create a copy of a tree structure.
- **Binary Tree Serialization**: Preorder traversal is used to serialize a binary tree into a sequence for storage or transmission.

**Postorder Traversal:**

In a Postorder traversal, you start from the root and traverse the tree by visiting the left subtree first, then the right subtree, and finally the root. The order is (left, right, root).

**Applications of Postorder Traversal:**

- **Memory Cleanup**: In some cases, Postorder traversal is used to deallocate memory occupied by nodes.
- **Expression Evaluation**: Postorder traversal is used to evaluate expressions stored in expression trees.

**Choosing the Right Traversal:**

The choice of traversal depends on the task you're trying to accomplish. For example, if you want to retrieve data in sorted order from a binary search tree, Inorder traversal is ideal. If you're trying to recreate a copy of a tree, Preorder traversal is useful.

**Recursive Traversal Approach:**

Recursion is a natural fit for binary tree traversal. For each traversal method, you write a recursive function that traverses the left subtree, then processes the root node, and finally traverses the right subtree.

**Iterative Traversal Approach:**

Traversing binary trees iteratively is also possible using stacks or queues. Iterative approaches can be more memory-efficient and can sometimes be advantageous when dealing with very large trees.

Binary tree traversal methods—Inorder, Preorder, and Postorder—provide essential techniques for navigating and processing binary tree structures. Each method offers unique insights into the tree's organization and facilitates various algorithms in fields such as expression parsing, data extraction, and memory management. Understanding these traversal methods equips you with the ability to manipulate and analyze binary trees efficiently, contributing to your skills as a data-driven developer.

## Binary Search Trees: Principles and Operations

Binary Search Trees (BSTs) are a specialized form of binary

trees that exhibit a powerful property: for each node, all nodes in its left subtree have smaller values, and all nodes in its right subtree have larger values. This property makes BSTs an excellent choice for efficient data storage, retrieval, and manipulation.

**Understanding Binary Search Trees:**

A Binary Search Tree (BST) is a binary tree in which each node follows the BST property. This property ensures that the value of each node is greater than all values in its left subtree and smaller than all values in its right subtree.

**BST Operations:**

1. **Insertion**: Adding a new element while maintaining the BST property.

2. **Search**: Finding a specific element in the tree efficiently.

3. **Deletion**: Removing a node while preserving the BST property.

**Advantages of Binary Search Trees:**

- **Efficient Search**: BSTs allow for quick retrieval of data by exploiting the BST property.

- **Ordered Data**: Elements are naturally ordered in a BST, facilitating range queries and sorting.

- **Dynamic Size**: BSTs can dynamically grow and shrink as data is inserted and deleted.

**BST Properties and Characteristics:**

- **Inorder Traversal**: Inorder traversal of a BST yields elements in sorted order.

- **Unique Elements**: BSTs only store unique elements;

duplicate values are not allowed.

- **Complexity**: Average-case time complexity for search, insert, and delete operations is O(log n) in a balanced tree. However, unbalanced trees can degrade to O(n).

**Balancing Binary Search Trees:**

Balanced BSTs ensure that the height difference between left and right subtrees is minimal, leading to improved performance. Various balanced tree structures, such as AVL trees and Red-Black trees, aim to maintain balance during insertions and deletions.

**Applications of Binary Search Trees:**

- **Dictionary Implementations**: Binary search trees are used to implement dictionaries, symbol tables, and associative arrays.
- **Auto-Complete Suggestions**: BSTs can assist in generating auto-complete suggestions based on user input.
- **File Systems**: Hierarchical file systems use BSTs to organize and locate files efficiently.
- **Database Indexing**: BSTs are used in indexing to accelerate data retrieval from databases.

**Choosing a BST Implementation:**

Selecting an appropriate implementation depends on the use case and the desired balancing properties. Self-balancing trees like AVL trees or Red-Black trees are preferable when maintaining balance is crucial.

Binary Search Trees offer an elegant and efficient way to

organize data with inherent ordering. By adhering to the BST property, these trees enable quick searches, insertions, and deletions. Their importance in applications ranging from dictionaries to databases underscores their significance in modern programming. Understanding Binary Search Trees equips you with a powerful tool for creating fast, ordered, and dynamic data structures, enhancing your ability to design and implement effective algorithms and systems.

# CHAPTER 11: ADVANCED TREE STRUCTURES

Welcome to the realm of advanced tree structures—a fascinating world where data organization becomes even more intricate and versatile. In this chapter, we'll explore advanced tree structures that build upon the concepts of binary trees, adding layers of complexity and power to your data manipulation arsenal. From balanced trees to heaps, we'll delve into these structures, their properties, and their applications.

## AVL Trees: Balancing for Better Performance

AVL trees are a remarkable advancement in the world of binary search trees, designed to maintain balance and ensure efficient performance for various operations. By enforcing a strict balance criterion, AVL trees provide logarithmic time complexity for search, insertions, and deletions, making them a powerful tool for managing ordered data.

## Understanding AVL Trees:

AVL trees are a type of self-balancing binary search tree. The term "AVL" stands for Adelson-Velsky and Landis, named after the Soviet mathematicians who introduced the concept. The core idea behind AVL trees is to maintain balance by ensuring that the height difference between the left and right subtrees of any node is no more than one.

## Maintaining Balance with Rotations:

When a new node is inserted into an AVL tree, balance may be disrupted. To restore balance, AVL trees employ rotation operations—single and double rotations—to adjust the tree's structure while preserving the BST property.

- **Single Rotation**: A single rotation is performed when a node's balance factor becomes greater than 1 or less than -1. Depending on the specific case (left-heavy or right-heavy), single rotations are either right rotations (LL) or left rotations (RR).

- **Double Rotation**: If a single rotation is not enough to restore balance, double rotations are applied. These involve a combination of two single rotations to bring the tree back to balance. There are two cases: left-right rotation (LR) and right-left rotation (RL).

## Properties and Benefits of AVL Trees:

1. **Balance Criterion**: In an AVL tree, for every node, the height difference between its left and right subtrees (the balance factor) is at most 1.

2. **Height-Balanced**: As a result of the balance criterion, AVL trees are height-balanced, ensuring logarithmic time complexity for various operations.

3. **Efficient Operations**: With logarithmic time complexity for search, insertions, and deletions, AVL trees are ideal for applications that require efficient data manipulation.

**Applications of AVL Trees:**

- **Databases**: AVL trees are used in database indexing to speed up data retrieval operations.

- **Symbol Tables**: AVL trees are employed in symbol tables, ensuring efficient storage and retrieval of keys.

- **Ordered Data**: Applications requiring ordered data storage and retrieval benefit from AVL trees' sorted structure.

**Drawbacks and Considerations:**

1. **Balancing Overhead**: Maintaining balance requires frequent rotations during insertions and deletions, which can impact performance.

2. **Memory Overhead**: AVL trees store extra balance factor information, increasing memory usage compared to regular binary search trees.

AVL trees exemplify the beauty of balancing in data structures, providing logarithmic time complexity for search, insertions, and deletions while ensuring a balanced hierarchical organization. By understanding the principles of AVL trees and their rotation operations, you'll be equipped to design and implement efficient data structures for applications that require ordered data storage and manipulation.

## Red-Black Trees: Maintaining Balance

Red-Black trees are a captivating data structure that combines the elegance of binary search trees with a clever coloring scheme to maintain balance efficiently. These self-balancing trees offer logarithmic time complexity for various operations while guaranteeing that the longest path in the tree is no more than twice the length of the shortest path.

### Understanding Red-Black Trees:

Red-Black trees are a type of self-balancing binary search tree that ensures balance by using a coloring scheme. Each node in a Red-Black tree is colored either red or black, and a set of rules governs the arrangement of colors to maintain balance.

### Maintaining Balance with Coloring:

Red-Black trees use five properties to ensure balance:

1. **Root Property**: The root is always black.
2. **Red Property**: Red nodes cannot have red children; every red node must have black children.
3. **Black Depth Property**: Every path from the root to any null (empty) leaf node must have the same number of black nodes.
4. **Double Black Property**: If a black node has two black children, it can be replaced with a double black node, which represents two black nodes in one.

5. **Leaf Property**: All null (empty) leaf nodes are considered black.

## Insertion and Deletion:

During insertion and deletion, Red-Black trees apply rotations and color adjustments to maintain balance. These operations ensure that the Red-Black properties are preserved while adjusting the tree's structure.

## Properties and Benefits of Red-Black Trees:

1. **Balanced Height**: Due to the color scheme and balancing rules, Red-Black trees maintain a balanced height, guaranteeing logarithmic time complexity for operations.

2. **Efficient Operations**: Red-Black trees offer efficient insertions, deletions, and searches, making them suitable for various applications requiring ordered data.

## Applications of Red-Black Trees:

- **C++ STL**: Many implementations of map and set data structures in C++'s Standard Template Library (STL) are based on Red-Black trees.

- **Database Indexing**: Red-Black trees are used to create indexes in databases, optimizing data retrieval.

- **Resource Management**: Red-Black trees help manage resources like memory blocks in memory allocators.

## Drawbacks and Considerations:

1. **Complexity**: Red-Black trees' complexity can be more challenging to implement and understand compared to simpler data structures.

2. **Memory Overhead**: The color information adds some memory overhead compared to regular binary search trees.

Red-Black trees exemplify the harmony between balancing principles and clever data structures. By using color coding and adhering to a set of properties, Red-Black trees maintain balance and ensure logarithmic time complexity for various operations. Understanding the intricacies of Red-Black trees equips you to design and implement efficient data structures for applications requiring ordered data manipulation and retrieval.

## B-Trees: Disk-Based Data Structures

B-Trees are an ingenious class of self-balancing tree structures optimized for efficient disk-based storage and retrieval of large datasets. With their ability to minimize disk I/O operations, B-Trees are a cornerstone in modern database systems and file systems.

### Understanding B-Trees:

B-Trees are designed with a focus on minimizing disk I/O operations, which can be a significant bottleneck in performance when dealing with large datasets stored on disk. These trees strike a balance between height and width, allowing them to store a substantial number of elements in each node, resulting in fewer levels in the tree.

### Balancing for Disk Efficiency:

Unlike binary search trees, B-Trees allow for multiple keys per node. The structure of a B-Tree involves the following properties:

1. **Balanced Structure**: B-Trees maintain a balanced height, ensuring efficient disk-based operations.

2. **Node Capacity**: Each node can contain a variable number of keys, optimized for disk page sizes.

3. **Ordered Keys**: Keys within a node are stored in a sorted order, facilitating efficient search operations.

**Insertion and Deletion:**

Inserting and deleting keys in a B-Tree involves redistributing keys within nodes and possibly splitting or merging nodes to maintain balance. These operations ensure that the B-Tree properties are upheld while optimizing disk-based access.

**Properties and Benefits of B-Trees:**

1. **Disk Efficiency**: B-Trees optimize disk I/O operations, making them ideal for applications requiring efficient data retrieval from disk-based storage.

2. **Height-Balanced**: The balanced height of B-Trees guarantees logarithmic time complexity for search, insertions, and deletions.

3. **Dynamic Size**: B-Trees can dynamically grow and shrink as data is inserted and deleted.

**Applications of B-Trees:**

- **File Systems**: B-Trees are used in file systems to manage large file hierarchies efficiently.

- **Databases**: B-Trees are employed in database systems to index and manage large datasets stored on disk.

- **Search Engines**: B-Trees help search engines manage large indexes for fast search operations.

**Drawbacks and Considerations:**

1. **Complexity**: B-Tree operations can be more complex than those of simpler tree structures due to the balancing requirements.

2. **Memory Overhead**: B-Trees maintain multiple keys per node, which can lead to higher memory overhead compared to binary trees.

B-Trees represent a sophisticated solution to the challenges of efficient disk-based storage and retrieval. By optimizing for disk I/O operations and maintaining a balanced height, B-Trees deliver logarithmic time complexity for various operations. Understanding B-Trees equips you with a crucial tool for designing systems capable of managing large datasets efficiently, enhancing your ability to work with data at scale.

## Heap Data Structure: Binary Heaps

Binary Heaps are a captivating and efficient data structure used for priority-based operations and sorting. These tree-like structures maintain a specific ordering property that allows for quick retrieval of the highest (max heap) or lowest (min heap) element.

**Understanding Binary Heaps:**

A Binary Heap is a complete binary tree with a unique property: for a max heap, the value of each node is greater than or equal to the values of its children, while for a min heap, each node's value is less than or equal to its children. This property ensures that the highest (or lowest) element is at the root, allowing for efficient access.

**Heap Operations:**

1. **Insertion**: Adding a new element to the heap while maintaining the heap property.

2. **Extract-Max (or Min)**: Removing and returning the highest (or lowest) element while maintaining the heap property.

3. **Heapify**: Converting an array of elements into a heap structure.

4. **Heap Sort**: Sorting an array using the heap data structure.

**Building and Maintaining the Heap:**

Binary Heaps are built using heapify operations that ensure the heap property is satisfied at each level of the tree. When elements are added or removed, the heap property is maintained through a process of "bubbling up" (up-heap) or "bubbling down" (down-heap) operations.

**Properties and Benefits of Binary Heaps:**

1. **Efficient Priority Operations**: Binary Heaps enable efficient retrieval of the highest (max heap) or lowest (min heap) element in constant time.

2. **Heap Sort**: Heap data structures facilitate heap sort algorithms with a time complexity of $O(n \log n)$.

3. **Priority Queues**: Binary Heaps are often used as the

underlying structure for priority queue implementations.

**Applications of Binary Heaps:**

- **Task Scheduling**: Binary Heaps are used to efficiently schedule tasks with varying priorities.

- **Graph Algorithms**: Algorithms like Dijkstra's shortest path and Prim's minimum spanning tree use binary heaps to select the next vertex efficiently.

- **Operating Systems**: Binary Heaps are used in memory management and scheduling algorithms.

**Drawbacks and Considerations:**

1. **Unordered Structure**: The heap structure doesn't provide any ordering between elements other than the max or min heap property.

2. **Limited Access**: While accessing the highest (or lowest) element is efficient, accessing other elements directly is not as straightforward.

Binary Heaps offer a powerful solution for priority-based operations and sorting, thanks to their efficient access to the highest (or lowest) element. By understanding their properties and operations, you'll be equipped to design and implement algorithms that rely on efficient priority-based data manipulation, enhancing your ability to optimize scheduling, graph algorithms, and more.

## Priority Queues: Implementation and Applications

Priority Queues are a versatile data structure that enables

efficient handling of elements with varying priorities. These structures allow for quick retrieval of the highest-priority element, making them valuable for applications ranging from task scheduling to graph algorithms.

**Understanding Priority Queues:**

A Priority Queue is a collection of elements where each element has an associated priority. The primary operation is to retrieve the element with the highest (or lowest) priority. Priority Queues abstract the concept of a queue, focusing solely on the order of priority.

**Implementations of Priority Queues:**

1. **Unordered List**: Simply maintaining a list and scanning for the highest-priority element when needed. However, this approach is not efficient for large datasets.

2. **Binary Heaps**: Binary Heaps, discussed earlier, provide efficient priority queue operations with logarithmic time complexity for insertion and extraction.

3. **Self-Balancing Trees**: Self-balancing binary search trees, like AVL trees or Red-Black trees, can be used to implement Priority Queues.

**Applications of Priority Queues:**

- **Task Scheduling**: Priority Queues are used to schedule tasks based on their priorities.

- **Dijkstra's Algorithm**: Finding the shortest path in graphs using Dijkstra's algorithm involves a Priority Queue to process vertices in order of their distance from the source.

- **Huffman Coding**: Priority Queues are used to build Huffman trees for efficient data compression.
- **Simulation Systems**: Priority Queues are employed in simulation systems to process events in the order of their occurrence time.

**Implementation Considerations:**

1. **Choosing the Right Implementation**: The choice of Priority Queue implementation depends on the specific application and the expected number of elements.
2. **Handling Tie Breakers**: If elements have equal priorities, additional logic is needed to handle tie-breaking scenarios.

Priority Queues offer an elegant solution for managing elements with varying priorities efficiently. By providing fast access to the highest-priority element, Priority Queues enhance the performance of various algorithms and systems. Understanding their principles and applications equips you with a versatile tool for optimizing task scheduling, graph algorithms, data compression, and more, ultimately enhancing your ability to design efficient and effective software systems.

# CHAPTER 12: GRAPHS AND GRAPH ALGORITHMS

Welcome to the exciting world of graphs and graph algorithms—an essential domain in computer science that models connections between entities and solves complex problems across various domains. In this chapter, we'll explore the fundamental concepts of graphs, their types, properties, and a range of algorithms that leverage graph structures to solve intriguing challenges.

## Introduction to Graphs

Graphs are a fundamental data structure used to model relationships between entities in various domains. They provide a powerful framework for representing connections, networks, and dependencies, making them a cornerstone of computer science and real-world applications.

**Graph Components:**

At its core, a graph consists of two main components:

1. **Vertices (Nodes)**: These are the entities or points in the graph. Each vertex can represent an object, a location, a person, or any other entity you want to model.

2. **Edges (Connections)**: Edges represent the relationships or connections between vertices. An edge connects two vertices and can be directional (from one vertex to another) or undirected (bidirectional).

**Graph Terminology:**

- **Adjacency**: Two vertices are adjacent if they are connected by an edge.

- **Degree**: The degree of a vertex is the number of edges connected to it.

- **Path**: A path is a sequence of vertices where each vertex is connected to the next by an edge.

- **Cycle**: A cycle is a path that starts and ends at the same vertex.

- **Connected**: A graph is connected if there is a path between any pair of vertices.

- **Weighted Graph**: In a weighted graph, each edge has a weight or value associated with it.

**Types of Graphs:**

Graphs come in various forms, each catering to different scenarios:

- **Undirected Graphs**: Edges have no direction, and connections are symmetric.

- **Directed Graphs (Digraphs)**: Edges have a direction, indicating asymmetric relationships.
- **Weighted Graphs**: Edges have weights, representing values or costs associated with connections.
- **Cyclic and Acyclic Graphs**: Cyclic graphs contain at least one cycle (loop), while acyclic graphs do not have cycles.
- **Connected and Disconnected Graphs**: A connected graph has a path between every pair of vertices, while a disconnected graph does not.

**Applications of Graphs:**

Graphs find applications in various fields due to their ability to model relationships and dependencies:

- **Social Networks**: Modeling connections between individuals in social media platforms.
- **Transportation Networks**: Representing routes and connections in road or flight networks.
- **Recommendation Systems**: Analyzing connections to make relevant recommendations.
- **Circuit Design**: Modeling connections in electronic circuits.
- **Data Analysis**: Graph algorithms can reveal patterns and insights in data.

Graphs provide a versatile and intuitive way to model relationships and connections in diverse scenarios. Understanding the basics of graphs—vertices, edges, types, and terminology—

lays the foundation for delving into more advanced concepts and algorithms. Graphs are not only a key element in computer science but also a tool for solving real-world problems, making them a fascinating and valuable area of study.

## Graph Representation: Adjacency Matrix and List

Graphs can be represented using different data structures, each with its advantages and trade-offs. Two common methods are the adjacency matrix and the adjacency list. These representations provide insights into the connections between vertices and determine the efficiency of graph algorithms.

**Adjacency Matrix:**

An adjacency matrix is a two-dimensional array that represents a graph's connections. Rows and columns correspond to vertices, and the matrix cells indicate whether there is an edge between vertices. In an unweighted graph, the matrix stores binary values (1 for connected, 0 for not connected). For weighted graphs, the matrix stores edge weights.

**Advantages of Adjacency Matrix:**

- **Direct Edge Information**: The presence or absence of an edge between any two vertices can be directly determined from the matrix.

- **Efficient for Dense Graphs**: In dense graphs (many edges), matrix operations can be more efficient.

**Disadvantages of Adjacency Matrix:**

- **Space Complexity**: The matrix consumes $O(V^2)$ space,

where V is the number of vertices, even if the graph is sparse (few edges).

- **Inefficient for Sparse Graphs**: For sparse graphs, most of the matrix entries are unused, resulting in wasted memory.
- **Slower for Large Graphs**: Matrix operations can be slower for large graphs due to memory access patterns.

**Adjacency List:**

An adjacency list represents a graph using an array of lists. Each vertex in the array has a corresponding list that contains its adjacent vertices. For unweighted graphs, these lists can be simple arrays or linked lists. For weighted graphs, the lists hold pairs of adjacent vertices and their corresponding edge weights.

**Advantages of Adjacency List:**

- **Space Efficiency**: Adjacency lists are more memory-efficient for sparse graphs since they only store information about existing edges.
- **Efficient for Sparse Graphs**: Accessing the adjacency list of a vertex takes O(degree) time, which is efficient for sparse graphs.
- **Dynamic Size**: Adjacency lists can be easily modified and resized as vertices and edges are added or removed.

**Disadvantages of Adjacency List:**

- **Slower Edge Queries**: Determining the presence of an edge requires searching the adjacency list, potentially taking longer than direct matrix access.
- **Memory Overhead**: In languages with object-oriented

overhead, storing each vertex's adjacency list can consume additional memory.

## Choosing the Right Representation:

The choice between an adjacency matrix and an adjacency list depends on factors such as the graph's density, the types of operations performed, and memory considerations.

The representation of a graph—whether through an adjacency matrix or an adjacency list—shapes the efficiency and performance of graph algorithms. Understanding the trade-offs between these representations is crucial for selecting the right one based on the specific graph structure, the type of operations to be performed, and the available memory resources.

## Breadth-First Search (BFS)

Breadth-First Search (BFS) is a fundamental graph traversal algorithm used to explore a graph layer by layer, starting from a chosen source vertex. This algorithm is invaluable for tasks like finding the shortest path, identifying connected components, and traversing graphs in a systematic manner.

### Principles of BFS:

BFS explores a graph by systematically visiting all vertices and edges in a breadth-first order. The algorithm explores vertices at the current level before moving to the next level. This ensures that the shortest paths are found first.

### BFS Process:

1. **Initialization**: Start by enqueueing (adding to a queue) the source vertex and marking it as visited.

2. **Exploration**: While the queue is not empty, do the following:

    - Dequeue a vertex from the front of the queue.

    - Explore its adjacent vertices (neighbors) that haven't been visited yet.

    - Enqueue these neighbors and mark them as visited.

3. **Termination**: Stop when the queue becomes empty, indicating that all reachable vertices have been visited.

**Applications of BFS:**

1. **Shortest Path**: BFS can find the shortest path from a source vertex to all other vertices in an unweighted graph.

2. **Connected Components**: BFS helps identify connected components in an undirected graph.

3. **Bipartite Graphs**: BFS can determine if a graph is bipartite (vertices can be divided into two sets with no edges between vertices of the same set).

4. **Crawl Web Pages**: BFS is used in web crawling to discover and index web pages.

**Advantages of BFS:**

- **Shortest Path**: BFS guarantees finding the shortest path in an unweighted graph.

- **Systematic Exploration**: BFS ensures systematic traversal of all vertices and edges.

**Disadvantages of BFS:**

- **Memory Usage**: BFS uses a queue to store vertices, which can consume significant memory for large graphs.
- **Inefficient for Deep Graphs**: BFS might not be efficient for deep graphs with many levels.

**Complexity of BFS:**

- Time Complexity: $O(V + E)$, where V is the number of vertices and E is the number of edges.
- Space Complexity: $O(V)$ for the queue used in BFS.

Breadth-First Search is a versatile algorithm for systematically exploring graphs and solving problems related to connectivity and shortest paths. By visiting vertices layer by layer, BFS ensures efficient and reliable traversal. Understanding the principles and applications of BFS equips you with a powerful tool for analyzing relationships, finding shortest paths, and tackling problems across various domains.

## Depth-First Search (DFS)

Depth-First Search (DFS) is a versatile graph traversal algorithm that explores a graph by visiting vertices as deeply as possible before backtracking. DFS is an essential tool for solving a variety of problems, including pathfinding, cycle detection, and analyzing connected components.

**Principles of DFS:**

DFS explores a graph by visiting a vertex and then recursively exploring its unvisited neighbors. It keeps going deeper until it reaches a dead end, after which it backtracks and explores other unvisited branches.

**DFS Process:**

1. **Initialization**: Start by choosing a source vertex and marking it as visited.

2. **Exploration**: For the chosen vertex, do the following:
   - Visit the vertex and mark it as visited.
   - Recursively explore its unvisited neighbors.

3. **Backtracking**: When the exploration of a vertex's neighbors is complete, backtrack to the previous vertex and continue exploring unvisited neighbors from there.

4. **Termination**: Stop when all vertices have been visited or the desired condition is met.

**Applications of DFS:**

1. **Pathfinding**: DFS can find paths between two vertices in a graph.

2. **Cycle Detection**: DFS can detect cycles in graphs.

3. **Connected Components**: DFS helps identify connected components in an undirected graph.

4. **Topological Sorting**: DFS is used to order vertices in a directed acyclic graph in a way that respects edge directions.

**Advantages of DFS:**

- **Memory Efficiency**: DFS typically uses less memory compared to BFS, as it doesn't require storing all vertices in a queue.

- **Solving Complex Problems**: DFS can be used to solve problems involving paths, cycles, and connectedness.

**Disadvantages of DFS:**

- **Completeness**: DFS might not visit all vertices in disconnected graphs if not implemented carefully.
- **Not Guaranteed to Find Shortest Path**: DFS doesn't guarantee finding the shortest path, as it may traverse longer paths before finding a shorter one.

**Complexity of DFS:**

- Time Complexity: $O(V + E)$, where V is the number of vertices and E is the number of edges.
- Space Complexity: $O(V)$ for the stack used in DFS recursion.

Depth-First Search is a powerful algorithm that allows you to explore graphs by delving deeply into paths and backtracking when necessary. By understanding the principles and applications of DFS, you'll be equipped to tackle a wide range of graph-related problems, from finding paths to detecting cycles and more. DFS is an essential tool in your arsenal for analyzing relationships, understanding connectivity, and solving problems across various domains.

## Shortest Path Algorithms: Dijkstra's and Bellman-Ford

Shortest path algorithms are essential tools for finding the most efficient paths between vertices in a graph. Two widely used algorithms for this purpose are Dijkstra's algorithm and the Bellman-Ford algorithm. These algorithms provide solutions for different scenarios and graph types.

**Dijkstra's Algorithm:**

Dijkstra's algorithm finds the shortest paths from a single source vertex to all other vertices in a non-negative weighted graph. The algorithm maintains a set of vertices with known shortest distances and repeatedly selects the vertex with the smallest distance to explore its neighbors.

**Dijkstra's Process:**

1. **Initialization**: Start with the source vertex and assign a distance of 0. Assign a distance of infinity to all other vertices.

2. **Greedy Selection**: Repeatedly select the vertex with the smallest distance from the set of unvisited vertices.

3. **Relaxation**: For the selected vertex, update the distances of its unvisited neighbors if a shorter path is found.

4. **Termination**: Stop when all vertices have been visited or when the target vertex is reached.

**Advantages of Dijkstra's Algorithm:**

- **Efficiency for Non-Negative Weights**: Dijkstra's algorithm works efficiently in graphs with non-negative edge weights.

- **Guaranteed Shortest Paths**: Dijkstra's algorithm guarantees finding the shortest path when edge weights are non-negative.

**Disadvantages of Dijkstra's Algorithm:**

- **Inefficiency for Negative Weights**: Dijkstra's algorithm doesn't work correctly with negative edge weights and might produce incorrect results.

- **Doesn't Handle Cycles**: Dijkstra's algorithm doesn't handle graphs with negative-weight cycles.

**Bellman-Ford Algorithm:**

The Bellman-Ford algorithm finds the shortest paths from a single source vertex to all other vertices in a graph, even when negative edge weights are present. The algorithm repeatedly relaxes edges to ensure that the shortest paths are found.

**Bellman-Ford Process:**

1. **Initialization**: Start by assigning a distance of infinity to all vertices except the source vertex (distance 0).

2. **Relaxation**: Repeatedly relax all edges in the graph $|V| - 1$ times, where $|V|$ is the number of vertices.

3. **Negative Cycle Detection**: After relaxation, check for negative-weight cycles. If any distance decreases in the $|V|$-th relaxation step, a negative-weight cycle exists.

**Advantages of Bellman-Ford Algorithm:**

- **Handles Negative Weights**: Bellman-Ford algorithm works correctly even when negative edge weights are present.

- **Detects Negative Cycles**: Bellman-Ford algorithm can detect negative-weight cycles in the graph.

**Disadvantages of Bellman-Ford Algorithm:**

- **Higher Complexity**: Bellman-Ford algorithm has a higher time complexity (O(V*E)) compared to Dijkstra's algorithm (O(V + E)).

Dijkstra's and Bellman-Ford algorithms play crucial roles in finding shortest paths in different types of graphs, considering various edge weight scenarios. Understanding their principles and applications empowers you to optimize route planning, network optimization, and resource allocation in real-world systems. Choose the appropriate algorithm based on the graph's characteristics and edge weight constraints to efficiently solve the shortest path problem.

## Graph Traversal and Connectivity

Graph traversal is a fundamental concept in graph theory that involves systematically exploring the vertices and edges of a graph. Traversal algorithms help us understand the structure of a graph, analyze its connectivity, and solve various problems.

**Types of Graph Traversal:**

1. **Breadth-First Search (BFS)**: Explores a graph layer by layer, starting from a source vertex.
2. **Depth-First Search (DFS)**: Explores a graph by visiting vertices as deeply as possible before backtracking.

**Graph Connectivity:**

Graph connectivity refers to how vertices in a graph are

connected through edges. Understanding connectivity helps us analyze relationships, identify connected components, and find paths between vertices.

**Connected Components:**

In an undirected graph, a connected component is a subset of vertices where each vertex is connected to at least one other vertex in the subset. Graph traversal algorithms like BFS and DFS help identify and label these connected components.

**Strongly Connected Components:**

In a directed graph, a strongly connected component is a subset of vertices where there's a directed path between any two vertices in the subset. Algorithms like Tarjan's algorithm and Kosaraju's algorithm help identify strongly connected components.

**Applications of Graph Traversal and Connectivity:**

1. **Social Networks**: Traversal helps identify clusters of friends or groups of people with common interests in social networks.

2. **Network Routing**: Traversal assists in finding optimal paths for data transmission in computer networks.

3. **Maze Solving**: Traversal algorithms can solve mazes by exploring paths systematically.

4. **Circuit Analysis**: Traversal can analyze electrical circuits to determine the flow of current.

**Connectivity and Pathfinding:**

Graph traversal algorithms also play a role in pathfinding— finding paths between vertices. BFS finds the shortest path in an unweighted graph, while Dijkstra's and Bellman-Ford algorithms find shortest paths in weighted graphs.

Graph traversal and connectivity are fundamental concepts that provide insights into the relationships and structure of graphs. Traversal algorithms like BFS and DFS help us understand connectivity patterns, identify clusters, and solve problems that involve finding paths. By mastering these techniques, you'll be better equipped to analyze and manipulate graphs, making them invaluable tools across a wide range of domains, from social networks to computer networks and beyond.

# CHAPTER 13: DYNAMIC PROGRAMMING

Dynamic Programming is a powerful technique for solving optimization problems by breaking them down into simpler subproblems and storing their solutions to avoid redundant computations. It's widely used in various fields, from algorithm design to economics. In this chapter, we'll explore the principles, process, and applications of Dynamic Programming.

## Understanding Dynamic Programming

Dynamic Programming (DP) is a powerful problem-solving technique used to solve optimization problems by breaking them down into smaller subproblems and efficiently solving each subproblem only once. DP is widely applied in various domains, from computer science to mathematics and economics.

**Principles of Dynamic Programming:**

Dynamic Programming is built on the idea of solving a complex problem by breaking it into simpler subproblems, solving each subproblem only once, and storing the solutions for later use. The technique is particularly useful when the problem exhibits overlapping subproblems and has an optimal substructure.

### Overlapping Subproblems:

A problem has overlapping subproblems if it can be broken down into subproblems that are reused multiple times during the solution process. DP aims to avoid redundant calculations by storing solutions to subproblems.

### Optimal Substructure:

A problem has an optimal substructure if an optimal solution to the problem can be constructed from optimal solutions to its subproblems. DP leverages this property to build solutions bottom-up or top-down.

### Steps in Dynamic Programming:

1. **Identify Subproblems**: Break down the problem into smaller, more manageable subproblems that can be solved independently.

2. **Define the Recurrence Relation**: Express the solution to the original problem in terms of solutions to the subproblems. This relation forms the basis for the DP solution.

3. **Memoization or Tabulation**: Implement DP using memoization (storing solutions to subproblems in a data structure) or tabulation (building a table of solutions) to avoid recomputation.

4. **Build the Solution**: Use the solutions to subproblems to

construct the solution to the original problem.

**Memoization vs. Tabulation:**

- **Memoization**: In this top-down approach, solutions to subproblems are stored as they are computed to avoid recalculating them later.

- **Tabulation**: In this bottom-up approach, solutions to subproblems are iteratively computed and stored in a table or array.

**Applications of Dynamic Programming:**

Dynamic Programming is used in a wide range of problems, such as:

- **Fibonacci Series**: Efficiently computing Fibonacci numbers.

- **Shortest Paths**: Finding the shortest paths in graphs.

- **Knapsack Problem**: Maximizing value within a weight constraint.

- **String and Sequence Alignment**: Comparing and aligning strings or biological sequences.

- **Optimal Binary Search Trees**: Constructing binary search trees to minimize search time.

**Advantages and Challenges of Dynamic Programming:**

**Advantages**:

- **Optimal Solutions**: DP guarantees optimal solutions by considering all possible subproblem solutions.

- **Efficiency**: By avoiding redundant calculations, DP significantly improves efficiency.

**Challenges**:

- **Memory Usage**: DP may require substantial memory for memoization or tabulation.

- **Problem Formulation**: Identifying subproblems and defining the recurrence relation can be complex.

Dynamic Programming is a versatile technique that allows you to solve complex optimization problems efficiently by breaking them into smaller, manageable subproblems. Understanding the core principles of DP, its applications, advantages, and challenges equips you with a powerful tool to tackle a wide range of problems, optimize algorithms, and devise efficient solutions in various domains.

## Memoization vs. Tabulation: Choosing Your Dynamic Programming Approach

Memoization and tabulation are two fundamental techniques used in Dynamic Programming to solve optimization problems efficiently. Both approaches aim to avoid redundant calculations by storing solutions to subproblems, but they differ in their implementation and advantages.

**Memoization:**

Memoization, also known as the top-down approach, involves solving a problem recursively by breaking it down into smaller subproblems. The solutions to these subproblems are stored in a data structure (usually a hash table) as they are computed, preventing duplicate calculations.

**How Memoization Works:**

1. Check if the solution to the current subproblem is already computed and stored.

2. If stored, return the stored solution; otherwise, compute the solution and store it for future use.

3. Recursively use stored solutions to solve larger subproblems until the original problem is solved.

**Advantages of Memoization:**

- **Selective Computation**: Memoization only calculates and stores the solutions that are needed, avoiding redundant calculations.

- **Elegance**: Recursive problem-solving structure often mirrors the problem's natural formulation.

**Challenges of Memoization:**

- **Recursion Overhead**: Recursive calls can lead to significant function call overhead.

- **Memory Consumption**: Storing solutions in a data structure can consume memory.

**Tabulation:**

Tabulation, also known as the bottom-up approach, involves solving a problem iteratively by building solutions to subproblems from the ground up. It uses a table (usually a 2D array) to store solutions to subproblems in a systematic order.

**How Tabulation Works:**

1. Initialize the table with base cases (solutions to smallest

subproblems).

2. Iteratively compute solutions to larger subproblems using solutions from already computed subproblems.

3. Build the final solution by using the stored solutions to subproblems.

**Advantages of Tabulation:**

- **No Recursion Overhead**: Tabulation eliminates the overhead of recursive function calls.

- **Efficient Iteration**: Tabulation uses a structured iteration pattern, making it more predictable.

**Challenges of Tabulation:**

- **Table Size**: Tabulation requires storing solutions in a table, which might consume more memory.

**Choosing Between Memoization and Tabulation:**

- **Memoization**: Use memoization when the problem has many overlapping subproblems and you want to avoid recomputation.

- **Tabulation**: Use tabulation when the problem's structure allows for an iterative approach, and you want to minimize recursion overhead.


Memoization and tabulation are both essential techniques in Dynamic Programming that enable efficient solution of optimization problems by avoiding redundant calculations. Choosing between the two depends on the problem's structure, the trade-off between memory consumption and computation time, and your coding preferences. By understanding the differences and advantages of memoization and tabulation, you can select the most suitable approach for solving a wide range of optimization problems.

## Solving Problems with Dynamic Programming

Dynamic Programming (DP) is a versatile problem-solving technique that can be applied to a wide range of optimization problems. By breaking down complex problems into smaller subproblems and storing their solutions, DP offers an efficient way to solve problems in various domains.

**Step-by-Step Approach to Solving Problems with DP:**

**1. Understand the Problem:**

- Clearly understand the problem statement, constraints, and objectives.
- Identify if the problem can be broken down into smaller overlapping subproblems.

**2. Identify Overlapping Subproblems:**

- Recognize if solving the same subproblem multiple times is wasteful.
- Determine if a recursive approach can be used to solve the problem.

**3. Define the Recurrence Relation:**

- Express the solution to the original problem in terms of solutions to subproblems.
- Formulate the recurrence relation that relates subproblems

to their solutions.

## 4. Choose Memoization or Tabulation:

- Decide whether to use the top-down (memoization) or bottom-up (tabulation) approach.
- Memoization stores solutions to subproblems in a data structure, while tabulation uses a table to store solutions.

## 5. Implement the Approach:

- Implement the chosen approach using recursion (for memoization) or iteration (for tabulation).
- Ensure that subproblem solutions are stored and retrieved efficiently.

## 6. Handle Base Cases:

- Identify and handle base cases—trivial subproblems that can be solved directly.
- These cases often serve as the starting point for building the solutions.

## 7. Build the Solution:

- Utilize the stored solutions to subproblems to construct the solution to the original problem.
- This step involves combining the solutions to subproblems in a way that follows the recurrence relation.

## 8. Analyze Time and Space Complexity:

- Analyze the time complexity of the DP solution, considering the number of subproblems solved.
- Evaluate the space complexity, accounting for the memory used by memoization or tabulation.

**9. Test and Validate:**

- Test the DP solution against various test cases to ensure correctness.
- Validate that the solution meets the problem's requirements and constraints.

**10. Optimize if Necessary:**

- Identify opportunities for optimization, such as reducing memory consumption or improving time complexity.
- Iterate on the solution to make improvements if needed.

**Applications of Dynamic Programming:**

Dynamic Programming is used to solve a wide variety of problems, including:

- **Fibonacci Series**: Efficiently compute Fibonacci numbers.
- **Shortest Paths**: Find shortest paths in graphs using algorithms like Floyd-Warshall and Bellman-Ford.
- **Knapsack Problem**: Solve optimization problems with weight and value constraints.
- **String and Sequence Alignment**: Compare and align strings or biological sequences.
- **Optimal Binary Search Trees**: Construct binary search trees to minimize search time.

Dynamic Programming provides a systematic approach to solving optimization problems by leveraging the principles of breaking problems into smaller subproblems and storing their solutions. By following the step-by-step process, understanding the concepts of memoization and tabulation, and practicing with a variety of problems, you'll develop the skills to efficiently tackle complex challenges across diverse domains.

## Examples: Fibonacci Sequence and Knapsack Problem

Let's explore two classic examples that demonstrate the power of Dynamic Programming: the Fibonacci sequence and the Knapsack problem. These examples showcase how Dynamic Programming can efficiently solve complex optimization problems.

### Example 1: Fibonacci Sequence

The Fibonacci sequence is a well-known mathematical sequence where each number is the sum of the two preceding ones. The sequence starts with 0 and 1: 0, 1, 1, 2, 3, 5, 8, 13, ...

**Problem Statement:** Given an index 'n', find the 'n'-th Fibonacci number.

**Dynamic Programming Solution:**

We can use DP to solve this problem efficiently using memoization.

1. **Base Case**: $F(0) = 0$, $F(1) = 1$.

2. **Memoization**: Store previously computed Fibonacci numbers to avoid redundant calculations.

3. **Recurrence Relation**: $F(n) = F(n-1) + F(n-2)$.

**Python Code:**

```
def fibonacci(n, memo={}):
    if n in memo:
        return memo[n]

    if n <= 1:
        memo[n] = n
    else:
        memo[n] = fibonacci(n-1, memo) + fibonacci(n-2,
memo)

    return memo[n]

n = 10
print(f"The {n}-th Fibonacci number is {fibonacci(n)}")
```

### Example 2: Knapsack Problem

The Knapsack problem is a common optimization problem where items with weights and values need to be selected to maximize the total value while staying within a weight limit.

**Problem Statement:** Given a set of items with weights and values, and a knapsack with a weight capacity, find the maximum value that can be obtained by selecting items to fit in the knapsack.

### Dynamic Programming Solution:

We can use DP to solve this problem using tabulation.

1. **Initialize Table**: Create a table to store the maximum value achievable for different weights and items.

2. **Base Case**: For weight 0 or no items, the value is 0.

3. **Tabulation**: Calculate the maximum value for each weight considering whether to include the current item or not.

### Python Code:

```python
def knapsack(weights, values, capacity):
    n = len(weights)
    dp = [[0 for _ in range(capacity + 1)] for _ in range(n + 1)]

    for i in range(1, n + 1):
        for w in range(1, capacity + 1):
            if weights[i - 1] <= w:
                dp[i][w] = max(values[i - 1] + dp[i - 1][w - weights[i
- 1]], dp[i - 1][w])
            else:
                dp[i][w] = dp[i - 1][w]

    return dp[n][capacity]

weights = [2, 3, 4, 5]
values = [3, 4, 5, 6]
capacity = 5

print(f"Maximum value that can be obtained:
{knapsack(weights, values, capacity)}")
```

The Fibonacci sequence and the Knapsack problem exemplify how Dynamic Programming can be applied to solve optimization problems efficiently. By breaking problems into smaller subproblems and storing their solutions, Dynamic Programming provides a systematic way to tackle complex challenges, making it a valuable tool across various domains.

# CHAPTER 14: GREEDY ALGORITHM

Greedy algorithms are a class of algorithms that make locally optimal choices at each step with the hope of finding a global optimum. They prioritize immediate gains without considering the consequences of those choices on future steps. In this chapter, we'll explore the principles, applications, advantages, and limitations of greedy algorithms.

## Introduction to Greedy Algorithms

Greedy algorithms are a class of problem-solving techniques that make locally optimal choices at each step with the hope of finding a global optimum. These algorithms prioritize immediate gains without considering the overall consequences of their choices. While they might not guarantee the best solution in all cases, greedy algorithms can be efficient and effective for solving certain types of optimization problems.

**Key Features of Greedy Algorithms:**

1. **Local Optimal Choices:** Greedy algorithms make choices that seem best at the current step, without considering their impact on future steps.

2. **Greedy Choice Property:** A problem exhibits the greedy choice property if a globally optimal solution can be achieved by making locally optimal choices.

**How Greedy Algorithms Work:**

1. **Initialization:** Start with an empty solution or initial state.

2. **Greedy Choice:** At each step, choose the best available option based on the greedy choice property.

3. **Update Solution:** Update the current solution by adding the chosen element or taking the selected action.

4. **Repeat:** Continue making greedy choices until a solution is constructed or a certain condition is met.

**Advantages of Greedy Algorithms:**

- **Efficiency:** Greedy algorithms are often efficient, as they don't require exhaustive search through all possibilities.

- **Simplicity:** Greedy algorithms are relatively simple to implement and understand.

**Limitations of Greedy Algorithms:**

- **Lack of Global Optimality:** Greedy algorithms do not guarantee finding the globally optimal solution for all problems.

- **Suboptimal Solutions:** Greedy algorithms may lead to suboptimal solutions if they make choices that seem best at each step but do not collectively result in the best overall solution.

**Determining the Applicability of Greedy Algorithms:**

Whether to use a greedy algorithm depends on the nature of the problem and whether it satisfies the greedy choice property. Consider the following factors:

1. **Greedy Choice Property:** Does the problem exhibit the greedy choice property? Can locally optimal choices lead to a globally optimal solution?

2. **Proof of Correctness:** Can you provide a proof that the greedy choices are indeed optimal in this problem?

3. **Optimality:** Are there alternative approaches (e.g., dynamic programming) that guarantee global optimality?

**Examples of Greedy Algorithms:**

- **Fractional Knapsack:** Choose items with the highest value-to-weight ratio to fill a knapsack with limited capacity.

- **Prim's Minimum Spanning Tree:** Build a tree with the minimum total edge weight that spans all vertices in a graph.

- **Kruskal's Minimum Spanning Tree:** Construct a minimum spanning tree by repeatedly adding the next lightest edge.

- **Activity Selection:** Choose a subset of activities to maximize the number of non-overlapping activities.

Greedy algorithms provide a simple yet powerful approach to

solving optimization problems by making locally optimal choices at each step. Understanding the principles behind greedy algorithms and their advantages and limitations equips you with the tools to apply this technique effectively to problems that exhibit the greedy choice property.

## The Greedy Choice Property

The essence of a greedy algorithm lies in its ability to make locally optimal choices at each step with the expectation that these choices will lead to an overall optimal solution. This property, known as the "Greedy Choice Property," is a fundamental aspect of greedy algorithms that allows them to make decisions that seem best in the short term without necessarily considering the bigger picture.

**Understanding the Greedy Choice Property:**

The Greedy Choice Property essentially states that at each step of the algorithm, the best immediate choice is made without considering its potential impact on future steps. This property allows greedy algorithms to focus on optimizing the current step based on the available options.

**Key Characteristics of the Greedy Choice Property:**

1. **Local Optimality:** Greedy algorithms prioritize the best available option at each step based on the immediate context, aiming for short-term optimality.

2. **Lack of Backtracking:** Once a choice is made, greedy algorithms rarely reconsider or backtrack, as their decisions

are based on the current state.

**Conditions for the Greedy Choice Property:**

For a problem to exhibit the Greedy Choice Property, it should satisfy two crucial conditions:

1. **Optimal Substructure:** The problem can be broken down into smaller subproblems, and the solution to the original problem can be constructed from the optimal solutions to these subproblems.

2. **Greedy Choice:** A globally optimal solution can be reached by making locally optimal choices at each step.

**Examples of Greedy Choice Property:**

- **Fractional Knapsack:** In the fractional knapsack problem, the Greedy Choice Property holds because selecting items with the highest value-to-weight ratio at each step leads to an optimal solution.

- **Dijkstra's Shortest Path:** Dijkstra's algorithm selects the vertex with the shortest distance from the source vertex at each step. This choice property helps find the shortest paths in a weighted graph.

**Advantages of the Greedy Choice Property:**

- **Simplicity:** Greedy algorithms are often straightforward to implement due to their focus on immediate optimality.

- **Efficiency:** Making locally optimal choices can lead to efficient solutions, especially when backtracking is unnecessary.

**Limitations of the Greedy Choice Property:**

- **Suboptimality:** Not all problems exhibit the Greedy Choice Property. Making the best immediate choice might lead to suboptimal overall solutions.
- **Counterexamples:** There are problems where making greedy choices at each step doesn't guarantee a globally optimal solution.

The Greedy Choice Property is a defining characteristic of greedy algorithms. By making locally optimal choices without the need for backtracking, greedy algorithms efficiently navigate through problems that satisfy the conditions of optimal substructure and the potential for globally optimal solutions. While not a guarantee of optimality in all cases, understanding and applying the Greedy Choice Property appropriately can lead to effective solutions for a variety of optimization problems.

## Examples of Greedy Algorithms

Greedy algorithms are versatile problem-solving techniques that find applications in a variety of optimization problems. They prioritize immediate gains at each step without considering long-term consequences, making them particularly useful for problems that exhibit the greedy choice property.

### 1. Fractional Knapsack Problem:

Given a set of items with weights and values, and a knapsack with a maximum weight capacity, the goal is to fill the knapsack with items to maximize the total value. In the fractional knapsack problem, items can be divided to fill the knapsack partially.

**Greedy Strategy:** Select items with the highest value-to-weight ratio first.

### 2. Huffman Coding:

Huffman coding is a compression algorithm used to encode characters with variable-length codes. It assigns shorter codes to more frequent characters and longer codes to less frequent characters to minimize the total encoding length.

**Greedy Strategy:** Build a Huffman tree by repeatedly merging the two least frequent characters.

### 3. Prim's Minimum Spanning Tree:

Given a connected, undirected graph with weighted edges, the minimum spanning tree (MST) is a tree that spans all vertices with the minimum total edge weight. Prim's algorithm constructs the MST by starting with a single vertex and iteratively adding the edge with the minimum weight that connects to the tree.

**Greedy Strategy:** Add the edge with the minimum weight that connects to the tree.

### 4. Kruskal's Minimum Spanning Tree:

Similar to Prim's algorithm, Kruskal's algorithm also finds the minimum spanning tree of a graph. However, it works by sorting all edges by weight and adding them to the MST if they don't create cycles.

**Greedy Strategy:** Add edges in ascending order of weight, ensuring that cycles are avoided.

### 5. Activity Selection:

Given a set of activities with start and finish times, the goal is to select a maximum number of non-overlapping activities that can be performed.

**Greedy Strategy:** Sort activities by finish times and select the one with the earliest finish time. Repeat with the next available activity.

### 6. Coin Change Problem:

Given a set of coin denominations and a target amount, find the minimum number of coins needed to make up the target amount.

**Greedy Strategy:** Choose the largest coin denomination that is smaller than or equal to the remaining target amount.

### 7. Job Scheduling with Deadlines:

Given a set of jobs with associated profits and deadlines, the goal is to schedule the jobs to maximize the total profit while meeting the deadlines.

**Greedy Strategy:** Sort jobs by profits and attempt to schedule them according to their deadlines, avoiding conflicts.

These examples demonstrate the diversity and versatility of greedy algorithms in solving various optimization problems. Greedy algorithms offer simplicity and efficiency when the greedy choice property applies, but careful consideration is necessary to ensure their correctness and optimality. By understanding the principles of these examples, you'll be better equipped to apply greedy algorithms effectively to a wide range of problems.

## Huffman Coding: Optimal Data Compression

Huffman coding is a widely used compression algorithm that efficiently encodes data by assigning shorter codes to frequently occurring characters and longer codes to less frequent characters. Developed by David A. Huffman in 1952, this technique has found applications in various areas, including file compression, data transmission, and image compression.

**Principles of Huffman Coding:**

Huffman coding achieves data compression by assigning variable-length codes to characters in such a way that the most frequent characters are represented by shorter codes, resulting in overall space savings. The core concept is to build a Huffman tree, where the paths from the root to each character's leaf node represent the binary codes.

**Steps to Construct Huffman Codes:**

1. **Frequency Count:** Calculate the frequency of each character in the input data.

2. **Priority Queue:** Create a priority queue (min-heap) of characters based on their frequencies.

3. **Building the Huffman Tree:** Repeatedly extract the two lowest-frequency characters from the priority queue, combine them into a new node, and insert the new node back into the priority queue. Continue until a single tree is formed.

4. **Assigning Binary Codes:** Traverse the Huffman tree from the root to each leaf, assigning '0' for a left branch and '1'

for a right branch. The resulting paths from the root to each character form their Huffman codes.

**Advantages and Significance:**

1. **Optimal Data Compression:** Huffman coding achieves the optimal data compression in terms of the number of bits required to represent each character. No other variable-length coding can achieve a shorter average code length.

2. **Variable-Length Codes:** Unlike fixed-length codes, such as ASCII, Huffman coding assigns shorter codes to more frequent characters and longer codes to less frequent characters, resulting in space savings.

3. **Reduced Storage and Transmission Costs:** Huffman coding reduces the size of data, making it ideal for storage and transmission, especially in resource-constrained environments.

4. **Fast Decoding:** Huffman coding provides fast and efficient decoding, as each code is uniquely decodable without requiring any lookahead.

**Example:**

Consider the phrase "HUFFMAN". The character frequencies are: {'H': 2, 'U': 1, 'F': 2, 'M': 1, 'A': 1, 'N': 1}. By constructing a Huffman tree, the resulting codes might be: {'H': '00', 'U': '01', 'F': '10', 'M': '110', 'A': '1110', 'N': '1111'}.

**Applications:**

1. **File Compression:** Huffman coding is used in various file compression formats, such as ZIP and GZIP, to reduce file

sizes.

2. **Network Data Transmission:** Huffman coding minimizes the amount of data to be transmitted, optimizing network bandwidth.

3. **Image Compression:** Huffman coding is part of image compression algorithms like JPEG, where it encodes frequency information.

Huffman coding exemplifies the effectiveness of greedy algorithms in achieving optimal data compression. By assigning shorter codes to frequently occurring characters, Huffman coding significantly reduces the space required for data storage and transmission. Its applications in various fields highlight its role in efficient communication and storage of digital information, making it a fundamental technique in the realm of data compression.

# CHAPTER 15: ADVANCED TOPICS AND REAL-WORLD APPLICATIONS

In the realm of data structures and algorithms, there's a wide array of advanced topics and real-world applications that extend beyond the fundamentals. These topics delve into more complex algorithms, specialized data structures, and applications that showcase the practical significance of mastering these concepts. In this chapter, we'll explore some of these advanced topics and their real-world applications.

## Disjoint Set Union (DSU) and Kruskal's Algorithm

The Disjoint Set Union (DSU) data structure and Kruskal's algorithm are powerful tools in the world of data structures and algorithms, particularly when it comes to solving problems related to graphs and spanning trees. DSU efficiently manages partitioned data sets, while Kruskal's algorithm finds the minimum spanning tree of a weighted graph.

## Disjoint Set Union (DSU):

DSU, also known as the Union-Find data structure, helps manage a collection of disjoint sets and efficiently performs operations like union (combining two sets) and find (determining the representative element of a set). DSU has a wide range of applications, including:

- **Connected Components**: Determining the connected components in an undirected graph.
- **Cycle Detection**: Detecting cycles in a graph during operations like Kruskal's algorithm.
- **Dynamic Connectivity**: Handling dynamic changes to connectivity in graphs.
- **Kruskal's Algorithm**: Efficiently implementing the union of sets during MST construction.

## Key Operations in DSU:

1. **Make Set**: Creates a new set with a single element.
2. **Find**: Determines the representative element (root) of a set.
3. **Union**: Combines two sets by connecting their respective representative elements.

## Kruskal's Algorithm:

Kruskal's algorithm finds the minimum spanning tree (MST) of a weighted, connected graph. An MST is a tree that spans all vertices of the graph with the minimum possible total edge weight. Kruskal's algorithm employs the DSU data structure to efficiently connect vertices while avoiding cycles.

## Steps of Kruskal's Algorithm:

1. **Sort Edges**: Sort all edges in ascending order of weight.

2. **Initialize DSU**: Create a DSU with each vertex as a separate set.

3. **Iterate Through Edges**: For each edge (u, v), if u and v belong to different sets (i.e., no cycle is formed), add the edge to the MST and perform a union operation in the DSU.

4. **Termination**: Continue until the MST contains (V - 1) edges, where V is the number of vertices.

**Applications of Kruskal's Algorithm:**

- **Network Design**: Finding the most cost-effective way to connect nodes in a communication network.

- **Cable Layout**: Planning the layout of cables or connections to minimize costs.

- **MST-based Algorithms**: Serving as a building block for various algorithms that require MSTs.

**Advantages of Kruskal's Algorithm:**

- **Greedy Approach**: Kruskal's algorithm is a greedy approach that constructs the MST by iteratively selecting edges with the smallest weight.

- **Efficiency**: The algorithm's efficient implementation using DSU ensures that cycles are avoided during MST construction.

Disjoint Set Union (DSU) and Kruskal's algorithm are invaluable tools in graph-related problems and minimum spanning tree construction. DSU efficiently manages connectivity and cycles, while Kruskal's algorithm effectively finds the minimum spanning tree of a graph. These concepts showcase how intelligent data structures and algorithms can elegantly solve complex problems and contribute to various applications across multiple domains.

## Topological Sorting

Topological sorting is a fundamental graph algorithm used to linearly order the vertices of a directed acyclic graph (DAG) in a way that respects the direction of edges. It has a wide range of applications, particularly in scenarios where tasks or events have dependencies and need to be executed or processed in a specific order.

**Principles of Topological Sorting:**

In a DAG, certain tasks or events depend on others to be completed before they can start. Topological sorting provides an order in which these tasks/events can be executed without violating any dependencies.

**Method of Topological Sorting:**

1. **Directed Acyclic Graph (DAG):** Start with a directed acyclic graph, where vertices represent tasks/events and edges represent dependencies.

2. **Indegree Calculation:** Calculate the indegree (number of incoming edges) for each vertex. Vertices with an indegree of 0 have no dependencies and are potential candidates for

starting the sorting.

3. **Queue-Based Approach:** Begin with vertices of indegree 0 and add them to a queue. For each vertex removed from the queue, reduce the indegree of its neighbors. If any neighbor's indegree becomes 0, add it to the queue.

4. **Order Construction:** As vertices are dequeued, they form the topological order.

**Applications of Topological Sorting:**

- **Task Scheduling**: In project management, topological sorting determines the order in which tasks should be executed to meet dependencies and deadlines.

- **Course Prerequisites**: When planning course schedules, topological sorting ensures that prerequisites are satisfied.

- **Compilation Order**: In software development, when one source file depends on another, topological sorting determines the order of compilation.

- **Data Dependency Analysis**: In optimizing compilers, topological sorting helps analyze data dependencies for parallel execution.

**Advantages of Topological Sorting:**

- **Directed Acyclic Graph Requirement**: Topological sorting works only for directed acyclic graphs, which fits many real-world scenarios where dependencies form a directed acyclic structure.

- **Efficiency**: The time complexity of topological sorting is linear, making it an efficient algorithm.

**Limitations of Topological Sorting:**

- **Cyclic Graphs**: Topological sorting is not applicable to graphs with cycles, as cycles introduce circular dependencies that cannot be linearly ordered.

- **Multiple Valid Orders**: In some cases, there can be multiple valid topological orders for a given DAG.

Topological sorting is a crucial algorithm that addresses the need to order tasks or events in a directed acyclic graph based on their dependencies. Its applications span various domains, from project management to software development, where tasks need to be executed or processed in a specific order. By leveraging the principles of topological sorting, you can effectively manage dependencies and optimize the execution of tasks in a wide range of scenarios.

## Trie Data Structure

A Trie (pronounced as "try") is a tree-like data structure used to store and efficiently retrieve a dynamic set of strings, such as words in a dictionary or keys in an autocomplete system. Tries are particularly useful for tasks involving string matching, prefix searching, and efficient storage of a large number of strings.

**Principles of Tries:**

Tries are designed to optimize the storage and retrieval of strings by organizing characters in a hierarchical structure. Each node in a Trie represents a single character, and a path from the root to a node forms a string.

**Structure of Tries:**

- **Root Node**: The top-level node, representing an empty string or the starting point.

- **Child Nodes**: Each node can have multiple child nodes, each corresponding to a different character.

- **Edges**: Edges between nodes are labeled with characters, forming the path to build a string.

- **Leaf Nodes**: Nodes with no children represent the end of a string, making them leaf nodes.

**Operations on Tries:**

1. **Insertion**: To insert a string into the Trie, traverse the Trie, adding nodes and edges for each character.

2. **Search**: To search for a string in the Trie, traverse it character by character. If the path exists, the string is present.

3. **Prefix Search**: To find all strings with a given prefix, traverse the Trie to the prefix and collect all descendants.

4. **Deletion**: To delete a string, remove its characters and nodes. Delete nodes with no children as well.

**Applications of Tries:**

- **Dictionary Implementation**: Tries efficiently store and retrieve words, making them suitable for dictionary implementations.

- **Autocomplete Systems**: Tries help provide suggestions in autocomplete systems based on prefix matching.

- **Spell Checkers**: Tries assist in finding valid words in spell checkers and correcting misspellings.
- **IP Address Lookups**: In networking, Tries can be used for fast IP address lookups.
- **Contact Lists**: Tries can be used to implement contact lists in phones, where searching by a prefix is common.

**Advantages of Tries:**

- **Efficient String Retrieval**: Tries allow for fast retrieval of strings with a time complexity proportional to the length of the string.
- **Prefix Searching**: Tries excel at finding all strings with a common prefix.
- **Space Optimization**: Common prefixes are shared among strings, reducing space consumption.

**Limitations of Tries:**

- **Space Consumption**: Tries can consume more memory compared to other data structures due to their hierarchical nature.
- **Complexity for Non-String Data**: Tries are best suited for strings and are not as intuitive for other types of data.

The Trie data structure offers a powerful solution for tasks involving dynamic sets of strings, such as searching, matching, and autocomplete. By organizing strings in a hierarchical manner, Tries provide efficient retrieval and storage mechanisms. Their applications range from word dictionaries to autocomplete systems, making Tries a valuable tool in string-related algorithms and applications.

## Searching in Rotated Sorted Arrays

Searching in a rotated sorted array is a common problem that involves finding a target element in an array that was originally sorted in ascending order, but has been rotated at an unknown pivot point. This scenario frequently arises in scenarios like searching in a rotated list of values or implementing search operations in rotated arrays.

**Challenges of Searching in Rotated Sorted Arrays:**

The rotation of the array introduces complexity to the search operation, as the normal binary search approach doesn't work directly. Special consideration is needed to determine the pivot point and adjust the search range.

**Techniques for Searching:**

There are a few approaches to efficiently search for a target element in a rotated sorted array:

1. **Binary Search with Modifications:** A modified binary search algorithm can be employed. While performing binary search, compare the mid-element with the start and end elements to decide which side of the array is sorted. Adjust the search range accordingly.

2. **Finding the Pivot Point:** To determine the pivot point (the point at which the array was rotated), a binary search variant can be used. The pivot point is where the element is

smaller than both its neighbors.

**Algorithms for Searching:**

1. **Modified Binary Search:**

    - Perform a binary search by considering the mid-element.

    - Compare the mid-element with the start and end elements to identify the sorted side.

    - Adjust the search range according to the sorted side.

    - Continue the search until the target element is found or the range is exhausted.

2. **Finding the Pivot Point:**

    - Use a binary search-like algorithm to find the pivot point.

    - Compare the mid-element with its adjacent elements to identify the pivot point.

    - Once the pivot point is found, determine which side of the pivot point the target element might be on and perform a binary search on that side.

**Applications:**

- **Search in Rotated Lists**: Applications where lists are rotated cyclically, such as rotating arrays to implement circular buffers.

- **Finding Minimum Element**: The pivot point often corresponds to the minimum element in the rotated array.

**Advantages:**

- **Efficiency**: Both algorithms have a time complexity of

O(log n), making them efficient for large rotated sorted arrays.

**Limitations:**

- **Sorted Arrays Only**: These algorithms are specifically designed for sorted arrays that have been rotated. They won't work for unsorted arrays.

**Conclusion**

Searching in rotated sorted arrays requires applying specialized techniques to account for the rotation. Modified binary search and finding the pivot point are effective strategies for tackling this problem efficiently. By understanding these algorithms, you can efficiently search for target elements in rotated sorted arrays and address real-world scenarios where such rotated lists or arrays are encountered.

## Handling Large Datasets and External Sorting

Dealing with large datasets that exceed available memory poses significant challenges in terms of storage, processing, and performance. External sorting is a technique used to efficiently sort and manage these datasets by utilizing external storage, such as hard drives or SSDs, rather than relying solely on the computer's main memory.

**Challenges of Large Datasets:**

Large datasets often surpass the available RAM, leading to the following challenges:

1. **Limited Memory**: Processing and sorting all data in

memory becomes impractical.

2. **Disk Access Latency**: Disk operations are slower compared to memory access.

3. **I/O Bottleneck**: Frequent disk reads and writes can create I/O bottlenecks.

**External Sorting Principles:**

External sorting addresses these challenges by splitting the dataset into smaller chunks that fit in memory, sorting them internally, and then merging the sorted chunks to create the final sorted dataset.

**Steps of External Sorting:**

1. **Splitting Phase**: Divide the large dataset into smaller chunks that can be sorted in memory.

2. **Internal Sorting**: Sort each chunk using an internal sorting algorithm like merge sort or quick sort.

3. **Merging Phase**: Merge the sorted chunks to produce the final sorted dataset.

**Benefits of External Sorting:**

1. **Efficient for Large Datasets**: External sorting allows sorting datasets that don't fit in memory.

2. **Reduced Memory Usage**: Smaller chunks are sorted internally, reducing memory requirements.

3. **Optimal Disk Access**: External sorting minimizes disk access by reading and writing data in an organized manner.

**Applications of External Sorting:**

1. **Database Systems**: Sorting large result sets from database

queries.

2. **Data Warehousing**: Handling large volumes of data for analysis and reporting.

3. **Log Files and Streaming Data**: Sorting logs or real-time data streams.

**Algorithms for External Sorting:**

1. **External Merge Sort**: Divides data into chunks, sorts them in memory, and then merges the chunks using multiple passes.

2. **Polyphase Merge Sort**: An extension of external merge sort with a more efficient merging strategy.

3. **Replacement Selection**: Uses a priority queue to select and merge runs of data.

**Considerations and Trade-offs:**

1. **Chunk Size**: Determining the optimal chunk size is crucial to balancing memory and disk access.

2. **Merge Strategy**: Choosing the appropriate merge strategy impacts performance and disk I/O.

3. **Buffer Management**: Efficiently managing buffers for reading, sorting, and writing is essential.

Handling large datasets through external sorting is a key strategy for efficiently processing and managing data that surpasses memory limits. By dividing the dataset into manageable chunks, sorting internally, and merging the results, external sorting optimizes disk access and provides a practical solution for scenarios involving large-scale data processing, storage, and analysis.

# CHAPTER 16: TIPS FOR PROBLEM SOLVING AND INTERVIEW PREP

Preparing for technical interviews, mastering data structures, and honing problem-solving skills are essential steps for success in the world of computer science and software engineering. This chapter provides valuable tips and strategies to help you navigate the interview process, tackle complex problems, and excel in technical interviews.

## Strategies for Problem Solving

Problem-solving is a core skill in computer science and beyond. It involves breaking down complex issues into manageable parts, devising effective solutions, and implementing them. Whether you're solving programming challenges, tackling real-world issues, or making informed decisions, effective problem-solving strategies are invaluable.

**1. Understand the Problem:**

Before diving into solving a problem, make sure you thoroughly understand it. Ask questions to clarify any ambiguities and define the problem's scope and constraints.

## 2. Divide and Conquer:

Break a complex problem into smaller, more manageable subproblems. Solving these subproblems can lead to solving the larger problem more easily.

## 3. Draw Diagrams and Visual Aids:

Use diagrams, flowcharts, graphs, and other visual aids to visualize the problem and its potential solutions. Visual representations can help you see patterns and relationships.

## 4. Algorithmic Thinking:

Develop a step-by-step plan or algorithm to solve the problem. Think about the logic and sequence of operations required to reach the desired outcome.

## 5. Work Backwards:

Start with the desired outcome and think backward, considering what steps or conditions are needed to reach that outcome.

## 6. Pattern Recognition:

Analyze the problem to identify any recurring patterns, similarities to known problems, or common approaches that can be applied.

## 7. Experimentation:

Try different approaches or test cases to gain insights into the problem. Experimentation can help you understand the problem better and discover potential solutions.

## 8. Use Examples:

Consider using concrete examples to illustrate the problem and potential solutions. Examples can clarify your understanding and guide your reasoning.

## 9. Research and Learning:

If the problem is unfamiliar, don't hesitate to research relevant concepts, algorithms, or techniques. Learning from others' experiences can provide valuable insights.

## 10. Abstraction:

Abstract the problem to its core elements, focusing on the essential components. This simplification can help you gain clarity and tackle the problem more effectively.

## 11. Revisit Similar Problems:

If you've encountered similar problems before, revisit your past solutions. Adapt and apply similar strategies to the current problem.

## 12. Collaborate and Discuss:

Discuss the problem with others—peers, mentors, or online communities. Different perspectives can provide fresh insights and solutions.

## 13. Time Management:

Allocate time wisely for understanding, planning, coding, and debugging. Setting time limits can help prevent spending too much time on a single aspect.

## 14. Debugging and Iteration:

If your solution doesn't work as expected, don't get discouraged.

Debugging is part of the process. Iterate, refine, and adjust your solution based on feedback.

### 15. Breaks and Rest:

If you're stuck, taking a break or sleeping on the problem can lead to new insights when you return with a fresh mind.

### 16. Practice Regularly:

Problem-solving is a skill that improves with practice. Regularly solve problems on coding platforms to hone your skills.

Effective problem-solving strategies empower you to tackle challenges methodically and efficiently. By understanding the problem, breaking it down, using visualization, and applying logical thinking, you can develop innovative solutions. Remember that problem-solving is a dynamic process that requires creativity, adaptability, and continuous learning. Whether you're writing code, addressing real-world issues, or making strategic decisions, these strategies can guide you toward successful outcomes.

## Cracking Technical Interviews

Technical interviews are a crucial part of the hiring process for many technology-related roles, such as software engineers, data scientists, and IT professionals. Cracking these interviews requires a combination of technical knowledge, problem-solving skills, and effective communication.

### 1. Master Fundamentals:

Solidify your understanding of core data structures, algorithms, and concepts. Review topics such as arrays, linked lists, trees, sorting, searching, and time complexity analysis.

### 2. Problem-Solving Skills:

Practice solving a variety of coding challenges on platforms like LeetCode, HackerRank, or Codeforces. Focus on different problem categories to enhance your versatility.

### 3. Data Structures and Algorithms:

Understand how various data structures (arrays, lists, trees, graphs) work and when to use them. Similarly, study different algorithmic techniques like sorting, searching, dynamic programming, and greedy algorithms.

### 4. System Design (For Senior Roles):

For senior roles, be prepared for system design interviews where you'll discuss designing complex systems. Understand concepts like scalability, load balancing, caching, and database design.

### 5. Interview Types:

Be ready for different interview formats, such as coding challenges, whiteboard coding, system design, behavioral questions, and technical discussions.

### 6. Practice Whiteboard Coding:

Practice coding on a whiteboard or paper to simulate the interview environment. Focus on explaining your thought process as you write the code.

### 7. Time Management:

Allocate time wisely during interviews. Don't spend too much time on a single problem; if you get stuck, move on and return later if time allows.

### 8. Ask Clarifying Questions:

When presented with a problem, clarify any doubts about the problem statement, input, and output requirements before attempting a solution.

### 9. Think Out Loud:

Explain your thought process as you solve problems. Interviewers often value your approach and reasoning more than a perfect solution.

### 10. Test Cases:

Test your solutions with multiple test cases to ensure they work correctly in different scenarios.

### 11. Soft Skills:

Practice active listening, ask follow-up questions, and engage in a friendly and professional manner. Good communication skills are vital.

### 12. Learn from Mistakes:

If you don't perform as well as you hoped in an interview, analyze your performance afterward. Identify areas for improvement and work on them.

### 13. Mock Interviews:

Conduct mock interviews with friends or mentors to simulate real interview scenarios. Get feedback to improve your performance.

### 14. Prepare Your Resume:

Highlight relevant experiences, skills, and projects on your resume. Be ready to discuss them in-depth during interviews.

### 15. Show Problem-Solving Process:

Even if you're not sure about a solution, demonstrate your problem-solving approach and logical thinking.

### 16. Keep Learning:

Stay updated on the latest industry trends, programming languages, and technologies. Demonstrating a growth mindset is impressive to interviewers.

Cracking technical interviews requires a blend of technical expertise, problem-solving skills, and effective communication. By mastering core concepts, practicing coding challenges, and simulating interview scenarios, you can increase your chances of success. Remember that interviews are not just about right answers but also about demonstrating your thought process, adaptability, and potential as a team member. With preparation, practice, and a positive attitude, you can navigate technical interviews confidently and land the role you desire.

## Commonly Asked Data Structure and Algorithm Questions

During technical interviews, interviewers often ask candidates to solve coding challenges that test their understanding of data structures, algorithms, and problem-solving skills. Being familiar with commonly asked questions and their solutions can significantly boost your interview preparation.

**1. Array Manipulation:**

Given an array of integers, find the maximum subarray sum.

**Solution:** Use Kadane's algorithm to find the maximum subarray sum by iterating through the array and keeping track of the maximum subarray sum ending at each index.

**2. Linked List Operations:**

Implement operations like adding elements, reversing, and detecting cycles in a linked list.

**Solution:** For adding elements, manipulate the next pointers. For reversing, iteratively reverse pointers while traversing. For cycle detection, use the Floyd's cycle detection algorithm.

**3. Binary Search Tree Validation:**

Determine if a given binary tree is a valid binary search tree.

**Solution:** Traverse the tree in-order and check if the values are in ascending order. Keep track of the previous visited node.

**4. String Manipulation:**

Given two strings, determine if one is a permutation of the other.

**Solution:** Count the frequency of characters in both strings and compare the frequency maps.

**5. Searching and Sorting:**

Implement binary search, merge sort, or quick sort algorithms.

**Solution:** Binary search divides the search space in half, while merge sort and quick sort sort arrays using divide and conquer techniques.

## 6. Graph Traversal:

Perform depth-first search (DFS) or breadth-first search (BFS) on a graph.

**Solution:** DFS uses a stack or recursion to traverse deeper into the graph, while BFS uses a queue to explore neighbors layer by layer.

## 7. Dynamic Programming:

Solve problems like the Fibonacci sequence or the knapsack problem using dynamic programming.

**Solution:** For Fibonacci, use memoization or bottom-up tabulation. For the knapsack problem, create a 2D table to store optimal solutions for subproblems.

## 8. Hashing:

Implement a hash map or solve problems related to duplicate detection.

**Solution:** Implement a hash map using an array and handle collisions with techniques like chaining or open addressing.

## 9. Stack and Queue Applications:

Solve problems involving stack and queue operations, such as balancing parentheses or evaluating expressions.

**Solution:** Use stacks for last-in-first-out operations and queues for first-in-first-out operations.

## 10. Recursion and Backtracking:

Solve problems involving recursive or backtracking approaches, like generating permutations or subsets.

**Solution:** Recursion involves breaking a problem into smaller instances of itself. Backtracking involves trying different paths and undoing choices when necessary.

Being familiar with commonly asked data structure and algorithm questions and their solutions can give you a strong foundation for technical interviews. Remember to understand the underlying concepts, practice different problem categories, and apply efficient algorithms. Additionally, focus on explaining your thought process clearly and consider optimization and edge cases in your solutions. With practice and a thorough understanding, you'll be better prepared to tackle a variety of coding challenges during interviews.

## Practicing on Online Coding Platforms

Online coding platforms have become invaluable resources for honing your coding skills, preparing for technical interviews, and staying updated on programming trends. These platforms offer a diverse range of coding challenges, real-world projects, and interactive learning experiences.

### 1. Diverse Problem Categories:

Online coding platforms offer challenges spanning various categories, such as data structures, algorithms, databases, machine learning, and more. This diversity helps you gain a comprehensive understanding of programming concepts.

### 2. Skill Building:

Consistent practice on coding platforms sharpens your problem-solving skills, algorithmic thinking, and coding proficiency. Regular challenges enhance your ability to tackle complex problems.

### 3. Realistic Interview Simulations:

Many coding platforms provide interview-specific challenges that mirror real technical interviews. Practicing these challenges prepares you for the types of questions you'll encounter during job interviews.

### 4. Learning from Solutions:

Platforms often showcase solutions from other users. Studying these solutions provides insights into different problem-solving approaches, coding styles, and optimization techniques.

### 5. Interactive Learning:

Interactive coding environments allow you to write and execute code directly on the platform. This hands-on experience fosters a deeper understanding of how code behaves.

### 6. Immediate Feedback:

As you solve problems, platforms often provide instant feedback on the correctness and efficiency of your solutions. This feedback helps you refine your approach and catch mistakes.

### 7. Collaboration and Community:

Online coding platforms host active communities where you can discuss problems, share insights, and seek assistance. Engaging with these communities can provide valuable learning opportunities.

### 8. Continuous Learning:

Many platforms offer courses, tutorials, and challenges related to emerging technologies and programming languages. This enables you to stay updated with industry trends.

**9. Progress Tracking:**

Platforms often track your progress, display your solved challenges, and recommend problems based on your skill level. This helps you set goals and monitor your growth.

**Tips for Effective Practice:**

1. **Start with Fundamentals:** Begin with foundational topics before moving to more complex challenges. Strengthening basics will build a solid programming foundation.

2. **Diverse Challenges:** Don't limit yourself to a single problem category. Explore different topics to broaden your skill set.

3. **Analyze Solutions:** After solving a problem, compare your solution with others to learn alternative approaches and best practices.

4. **Time Management:** Set time limits for challenges to simulate real interview conditions and improve your speed.

5. **Read Problem Statements Carefully:** Understand problem requirements and constraints before attempting a solution.

6. **Practice Regularly:** Consistency is key. Dedicate a specific time each day or week to practice on coding platforms.

7. **Experiment with New Techniques:** As you grow more

comfortable, experiment with new algorithms, data structures, and optimization techniques.

8. **Learn from Mistakes:** Embrace errors as learning opportunities. Analyze your mistakes and seek improvement.

Online coding platforms offer a rich ecosystem for continuous learning and growth in the world of programming. By practicing diverse challenges, engaging with the coding community, and consistently refining your skills, you can enhance your problem-solving abilities and excel in technical interviews. As you progress through challenges and courses, you'll become a more confident and capable programmer, equipped to tackle a wide array of coding challenges and real-world projects.

# PYTHON STANDARD LIBRARY FOR DATA STRUCTURES AND ALGORITHMS

Python's rich standard library includes a variety of modules that provide efficient implementations of data structures and algorithms. Leveraging these built-in tools can significantly simplify your coding tasks and enhance your problem-solving capabilities.

**1. collections Module:**

This module provides specialized container data types beyond the built-in ones, including:

- **deque**: A double-ended queue for efficient pop and append operations.
- **Counter**: Counts elements in an iterable and provides convenient access to frequencies.
- **defaultdict**: A dictionary with default values for missing keys.
- **OrderedDict**: A dictionary that remembers the order of

key insertion.

## 2. heapq Module:

The **heapq** module implements a heap queue algorithm, commonly known as a priority queue. It's useful for maintaining a priority queue in various algorithms.

## 3. itertools Module:

The **itertools** module offers fast, memory-efficient tools for working with iterators, including:

- **permutations** and **combinations**: Generate all possible permutations and combinations.
- **chain**: Chain multiple iterables together.
- **cycle**: Infinitely cycle through an iterable.
- **product**: Calculate the Cartesian product of multiple iterables.

## 4. math Module:

The **math** module provides mathematical functions, including:

- **factorial, sqrt, pow**: Common mathematical operations.
- **ceil** and **floor**: Rounding up and down, respectively.

## 5. functools Module:

The **functools** module contains higher-order functions and operations on callable objects, including:

- **reduce**: Apply a function to elements in a sequence cumulatively.
- **lru_cache**: Decorator for memoizing function calls with limited cache size.

## 6. bisect Module:

The **bisect** module implements binary search and insertion into sorted lists. It's helpful for maintaining ordered data and performing efficient searches.

### 7. datetime Module:

The **datetime** module provides classes for working with dates and times, which can be useful for algorithms involving time-based data.

### 8. random Module:

The **random** module offers functions to generate random numbers, useful for simulations and randomized algorithms.

### 9. re Module:

The **re** module provides support for regular expressions, allowing you to perform advanced string manipulations and pattern matching.

### 10. string Module:

The **string** module contains constants and functions for working with strings. It's useful for manipulating strings and characters.

### 11. sys Module:

The **sys** module provides access to some variables used or maintained by the interpreter and functions that interact with the interpreter.

### 12. time Module:

The **time** module provides various time-related functions, including measuring execution times and creating time delays.

Python's standard library offers a treasure trove of data

structures and algorithms that can simplify your coding efforts and streamline your problem-solving process. By becoming familiar with these modules and their capabilities, you can efficiently implement various algorithms and leverage powerful data structures without the need for external libraries. These modules not only save time but also enhance code readability and maintainability.

# GLOSSARY

This glossary provides definitions and explanations of key terms and concepts related to data structures and algorithms.

**Algorithm:** A step-by-step set of instructions or rules for performing a specific task or solving a problem.

**Array:** A data structure that stores a collection of elements, each identified by an index or a key.

**Binary Search:** A search algorithm that efficiently finds the position of a target value within a sorted array by repeatedly dividing the search range in half.

**Data Structure:** A way of organizing and storing data to perform operations efficiently. Examples include arrays, linked lists, trees, and graphs.

**Dynamic Programming:** A technique used to solve complex problems by breaking them down into simpler subproblems and storing the solutions to avoid redundant calculations.

**Hash Table:** A data structure that stores key-value pairs and provides fast access to values based on their associated keys.

**Linked List:** A linear data structure that consists of nodes, where each node points to the next node in the sequence.

**Recursion:** A programming technique where a function calls itself to solve a problem by solving smaller instances of the same problem.

**Sort Algorithm:** An algorithm that arranges elements in a specific order, such as ascending or descending.

**Stack:** A linear data structure that follows the Last-In-First-Out (LIFO) principle, where the last element added is the first to be removed.

**Queue:** A linear data structure that follows the First-In-First-Out (FIFO) principle, where the first element added is the first to be removed.

**Time Complexity:** A measure of the amount of time an algorithm takes to run as a function of the input size.

**Space Complexity:** A measure of the amount of memory an algorithm uses as a function of the input size.

**Tree:** A hierarchical data structure that consists of nodes connected by edges, with one node as the root and the remaining nodes forming subtrees.

**Graph:** A collection of nodes (vertices) and edges that connect pairs of nodes. Graphs can be directed or undirected.

**Queue:** A linear data structure that follows the First-In-First-Out (FIFO) principle, where the first element added is the first to be removed.

**Hashing:** A technique that converts data (such as a string) into a fixed-size value (hash code), often used in data storage and retrieval.

**Priority Queue:** A data structure that maintains a collection of elements with assigned priorities, allowing efficient access to the highest-priority element.

**Search Algorithm:** An algorithm that seeks to find a specific element or value within a collection of data.

**Big O Notation:** A notation used to describe the upper bound of an algorithm's time or space complexity in relation to its input size.

**Binary Tree:** A type of tree structure in which each node has at most two children.

**Traversal:** The process of visiting all nodes in a data structure or graph.

**Graph:** A collection of nodes (vertices) and edges that connect pairs of nodes. Graphs can be directed or undirected.

**DFS (Depth-First Search):** A graph traversal algorithm that explores as far as possible along each branch before backtracking.

**BFS (Breadth-First Search):** A graph traversal algorithm that explores all the neighbors of a node before moving on to their children.

**Memoization:** A technique of storing and reusing already computed results to avoid redundant calculations in recursive algorithms.

**Greedy Algorithm:** An algorithm that makes locally optimal choices at each step with the hope of finding a global optimum.

**Dynamic Programming:** A technique used to solve complex problems by breaking them down into simpler subproblems and storing the solutions to avoid redundant calculations.

**Binary Search Tree (BST):** A binary tree where each node has a value greater than all values in its left subtree and less than all values in its right subtree.

**Heap:** A specialized tree-based data structure that satisfies the heap property, often used to implement priority queues.

**Hash Map:** A data structure that stores key-value pairs and provides fast access to values based on their associated keys.

**Trie:** A tree-like data structure that is used to store a dynamic set of strings and provides efficient string search operations.

**DFS (Depth-First Search):** A graph traversal algorithm that explores as far as possible along each branch before backtracking.

**BFS (Breadth-First Search):** A graph traversal algorithm that explores all the neighbors of a node before moving on to their children.

**Collision Resolution:** Techniques used in hash tables to handle situations where two keys map to the same hash value.

**Standard Library:** A set of pre-written functions and modules available in a programming language for various common tasks and operations.

This glossary provides definitions for essential terms and concepts related to data structures and algorithms. Understanding these terms will help you navigate discussions, study materials, and technical interviews with greater clarity.

www.ingramcontent.com/pod-product-compliance
Lightning Source LLC
LaVergne TN
LVHW051227050326
832903LV00028B/2279